Emotional

Blocks

to

Learning

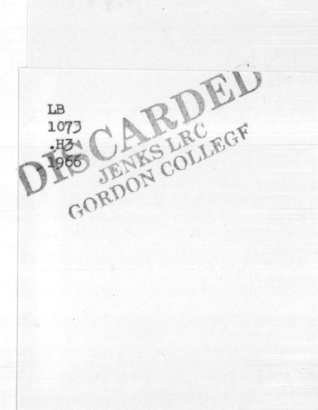

EMOTIONAL

BLOCKS

TO

LEARNING

A Study of the Reasons for Failure in School

IRVING D. HARRIS, M.D.

THE FREE PRESS, *New York*
COLLIER-MACMILLAN LIMITED, *London*

Collier-Macmillan Canada, Ltd., Toronto, Ontario

Library of Congress Catalog Card Number: 60-13779

FIRST FREE PRESS PAPERBACK EDITION 1966

SECOND PRINTING AUGUST 1966

To Tobie

ACKNOWLEDGMENTS

MY PRINCIPAL indebtedness is to the many workers whose observations supplied the basic data for this study. They include the present and past members of the Departments of Psychology, Social Service, and Psychiatry at the Illinois Institute for Juvenile Research, as well as teachers from the Chicago and suburban school systems. Without their contributions this study would not have been possible.

Certain other persons were also especially helpful. Dr. Raymond Robertson, Superintendent of the Institute, was encouraging both by his faith and by his supplying of necessary funds. Dr. Gustavo Lage, Medical Director of the Healy Residential School, enabled me to conduct and participate in a seminar on learning problems. In that seminar, I learned much from the Principal of the Healy School, Miss Kay Wimmer, as well as from the other members of the teaching staff. The arduous preparation of the manuscript was facilitated by the generous help of Mrs. Lillian Davis. I have appreciated the suggestions of the several persons who read the manuscript. In this connection, I found the critical reaction of Helen Robinson to be particularly useful. Finally, the intangible warm support provided me by my wife and children was indispensable in carrying the study and the book to a conclusion.

CONTENTS

Contents

Emotional

Blocks

to

Learning

i

*t*HIS BOOK is about an educational problem which is like
a tug of war. At one end of the rope is a schoolboy with adequate intelligence who is failing in his studies. For reasons of
his own, he views the learning situation with varying degrees
of anxiety and resentment. At the other end is a teacher. She
has attempted to pull and stimulate the boy but has failed.
She stands perplexed and frustrated, still hoping to induce him
to enter the land of learning.

It would be highly convenient if we could take one boy as
an example of all learning problems and devote the remainder
of the book to an examination of what happens within him and
within his family to make him so reluctant to learn. Though
his story would provide a simple unitary theme, it would give a
very false picture of the situation—for there are several kinds of
learning problems and several kinds of causes for them.

We can begin by discussing George, a boy much like the
one we have described. He is aggressive, is constantly interfering with his classmates' activities, and is occasionally defiant
toward the teacher. He appears deliberately to avoid studying
and finishing his assignments. Though he is repeating this grade,
he is failing in all subjects.

Another boy, Fred, exemplifies different problems. He acts
much younger than his years and has a speech defect. On the

surface, he seems not belligerent but helpless. He often brings his toys to school; sometimes he sits under his desk; and he will work only if the teacher stands over him.

Arthur, on the other hand, is a quiet, polite boy whose behavior gives no trouble in the classroom. He seems to like school and to be eager to learn. However, though he is in the fourth grade, he is still trying to master first grade reading. In other subjects, he does reasonably well.

Our last example, Tom, especially intrigues and perplexes the teacher. From some of his recitations and written assignments, and from his superior score on the intelligence test, she is sure that he has considerable intellectual potential. These intellectual flashes are, however, over-balanced by long stretches of listless, indifferent schoolwork. Frequently, Tom looks out of the window or daydreams instead of concentrating on his school work.

Our study of the boys begins after their teachers have used the resources of the school system—special tutoring, conferences with the guidance counselor, etc.—and have talked with the parents. The teachers have found that most parents are at their end of the rope in this tug of war. The parents, too, have usually tried coaxing, pushing, and even mental pounding. Sometimes in desperation, however, they have turned against the teachers. They have thought that the teachers have not presented the right incentives, have not pushed their sons hard enough or given them sufficient individual attention. A frequent result of this impasse is that the boy and his parents are referred to a child guidance clinic where more specialized help is available.

This book really begins at the clinic. The one we describe is the Illinois Institute for Juvenile Research. The author is a psychoanalyst who, for the past fifteen years has been a consultant at the Institute. From this opportunity to view a number of children with learning problems, he has been provided with two impressive statistics. First, that difficulty in learning was the most commonly encountered symptom at this clinic, which sees almost a thousand children a year; second, that this symptom occurred almost seven times more frequently in boys than in girls.

The widespread nature of this problem and its particular impact on boys led the author to study the clinical records of 100 boys—ages seven to sixteen—with at least average intelligence (minimum I.Q. of 90) who had been referred to the Institute *primarily* because of a learning problem. The aim, of course, was to discover why these boys did not learn. From this part of the study emerged some impressions that were so familiar and self-evident that they could be called truisms. Thus, it was found that the boys did not learn because they were emotionally disturbed, and that the reasons for their emotional disturbance could be traced to unfavorable home conditions.

The obviousness of these conclusions pointed up the fact that the important question was not *whether* these boys were emotionally disturbed but rather *what kind* of disturbance they had. We know that emotional disturbance does not always lead to learning difficulties. The very able, but very tense executive is more often affected in his arteries or his stomach than in his mental powers. Similarly, the other crucial question was not *whether* the home conditions were unfavorable but in *what particular* way they were unfavorable for learning. This question was evident since many boys who were referred to the Institute came from disturbed home situations but did not have learning problems.

The following two examples illustrate the necessity for being more specific about the causes for learning difficulties:

(1) Albert is a nine-and-a-half-year-old boy who, according to his mother, had a very difficult childhood. The parents separated when he was five-and-a-half and his grandparents moved in with his mother and him. The grandparents argued almost constantly in Albert's presence. The feeding problems he already had were accentuated by their quarrels at the dinner table.

He was always very restless and tense, and would go into tantrums, crying profusely, if he could not get his way. Once he came to his mother complaining that he was always cutting his index finger and wished to have it amputated. His I.Q. on the Stanford-Binet Test was 112.

(2) Frank is another nine-and-a-half-year-old. His mother reports that he is very disobedient at home, and that he has a temper tantrum if he cannot have his own way, or does just the opposite of what he is asked. He is especially belligerent towards his younger sister. His mother is afraid he will be a teen-age killer when he grows older. The mother and father get along rather well, although the mother's parents did not. His I.Q. on the Stanford-Binet Test was 108.

Now the question is: Which emotionally disturbed boy has the learning difficulty—Albert, or Frank? From these few facts about the boys and their family situation, they both seemed disturbed enough to have some repercussions in terms of their ability to learn at school. But, in fact, Frank has a learning difficulty and Albert has not.

Frank's school report reads: "Frank repeated grade 1-2, has done poorly since. He is failing in reading, spelling, composition, and social studies, and is now in an ungraded room." His teacher states:

In my opinion, Frank's greatest problem is a deep-seated feeling of inadequacy and inferiority. His behavior pattern runs a regular course: he is aggressive to strangers, belittles others' success, and is extremely sensitive to others' approval or disapproval. He disturbs other children, makes excessive demands for attention, and is frequently impudent and stubborn.

Albert's school report, on the other hand, reads simply:

Albert is not a problem; in fact, he is a very co-operative pupil and a desirable student. He is doing above average work in reading and social studies, and average work in spelling and arithmetic.

This study was undertaken to discover why Frank and not Albert should have had difficulty in learning. For this purpose, the clinical records of 100 consecutive boys similar to Albert were read. These boys were *like* the 100 boys with learning problems in that they were emotionally disturbed enough to be referred to a child guidance clinic, in that they also had at least average intelligence, and in that their ages ranged from seven to sixteen. They were *different* in that they had no significant difficulty in learning and in that they were referred to the clinic for such *primary* reasons as bed-wetting, nervousness, and difficulty in making friends. These boys (called the "learners") were compared with the first 100 boys (called the "non-learners") to find out the *kind* of emotional difficulties and the *kind* of unfavorable home conditions present. It is this comparison with which the book is mainly concerned, and from this comparison issued impressions which appear to be more fruitful than the truisms previously mentioned.

Let us examine the two groups a little more closely. All the boys in the non-learner group are not like Frank. Compared to the four boys described earlier, Frank is much like George, the aggressive boy. However, teachers also referred Fred, who is immature and helpless; Arthur, who is polite and submissive and who has a specific reading problem; and Tom, who day dreams. All were sent because they had learning difficulties. Since there are several kinds of learning problems, there may be several kinds of causes for difficulties in learning. In the forthcoming chapters, evidence is submitted which indicates that the reasons for daydreaming are not necessarily the same as those for low average intelligence or for difficulty in reading.

What is the "learner" group like? To answer this, we need not inquire further into the variety of presenting symptoms such as bed-wetting or nervousness. But we do need to describe the learners' educational performances more fully. None of these boys has ever had to repeat a grade; none is presently failing or barely passing in his subjects; none has had to have special help in reading or arithmetic. In short, none of these boys presents a learning symptom of sufficient magnitude that the teacher or parents have been impelled to seek help for him.

However, interesting differences occur within the learner group. While the majority of the boys received a clean bill of academic health from the teacher, a minority were reported to have symptoms that indicated a mild or potential learning difficulty. Typical of comments by their teachers were: "Not working up to full intellectual capacity" or "occasionally daydreams or has difficulty in concentrating." The relationship of these statements to learning difficulties is indicated by the fact that similar statements were made about the great majority of non-learners. For a while, the author debated whether or not to include these boys in the learner group. As we shall see, their final inclusion among the learners aided in reaching the conclusion that the same family factors which produced major learning problems also produced embryonic learning difficulties.

It is these family factors with which Part One deals. We shall consider the effects upon learning resulting from (1) the social class of the boy, (2) the disorganization of the family, (3) the ambitiousness of the parents, particularly the mother, (4) the degree of maturity expected of the boy by the parents, and (5) the role of aggression in learning. These, of course, do not represent all the possible influences issuing from the family. But they do represent those influences which were found, in this particular study of 200 boys, ages seven to sixteen, to differentiate the non-learners from the learners.

As far as possible, we shall try, using family factors, to show not only how learners differ from non-learners, but also how one kind of non-learner differs from another. Thus, in addition to such questions as whether the social class of the learner tends to be different from that of the non-learner, we shall be interested in asking whether the effect of social class will show up in the form of low-average intelligence, in daydreaming, or in reading problems. And whether the effect of family disorganization upon non-learners will be different from the effect of the mother's ambitiousness.

In Part Two, the points stressed in the first section will be further illustrated. While we shall consider no additional issues, the sources of case material will be new. We shall no longer be confined to the study group with its particular age range and diagnostic nature. Thus, in this section, one chapter is devoted to the cases of three young men who, despite superior intelligence, failed in college; one chapter, to the learning and behavior problems of two pre-schoolers; and the last, to a detailed account of a ten-year-old boy who spent four years in a residential school. Because all of these six cases were seen in a treatment setting, much more information is available about the factors involved in learning.

Part Three is concerned with a theoretical integration of what has been previously set forth and with practical implications. The first of these final two chapters deals with relating these study findings to the contributions of other investigators. It is somewhat technical and complicated and may be omitted by those readers who are not particularly interested in theory. The last chapter begins with a brief summary of all preceding chapters and discusses what the teacher and parent can and cannot do about learning problems. In the Appendices will be found most of the details about method and statistical results.

Since this book is intended for parents and teachers as well as clinicians, the language has been kept as free of technical terms as possible. Similarly, wherever the choice was open to discuss a topic on a simple or a complex level, the former alternative was taken. As a result, to the knowledgeable specialist there will occasionally appear to be some over-simplification. To combat this hazard, references are supplied which can further inform the reader about the complexities of the subject.

The kind of investigation made by the author is perhaps best described as an exploratory study in which observations were made, subjected to statistical treatment, and then integrated in the form of generalizations. It began with a question, "What are the psychological or emotional specifics in learning problems as seen in a sample of 100 consecutive cases?" rather than with an explicit hypothesis to be tested by experimentation. Though much of the original data had been collected by social workers, psychologists, teachers, and other psychiatrists, the reviewing, abstracting, and interpreting of their original observations were done solely by the author. The study depends to a considerable extent on what the author noted and how he interpreted the observations. This use of subjective judgment or taste is, as W. I. B. Beveridge says, inevitable and necessary in much scientific thinking.[1]* Because of its presence, every declarative statement in the book should be accompanied by qualifications. In order to preserve readability, this has not been done. It is hoped that a blanket qualification at this point will serve the purpose.

The author's viewpoint is that of a child psychiatrist with psychoanalytic training and experience. Because of this, certain factors will be emphasized more than others. If the author were a neurologist or a pediatrician, he would place more emphasis on such obstacles to learning as brain damage, visual and auditory defects, and malnutrition. If he were a psychologist, he would give more weight to tests which measure and classify intellectual abilities. The particular emphasis in this book, however, is on the emotional stresses which interfere with the boy's learning performance.

Moreover, this book differs in one important respect from others with a psychoanalytic orientation. The great majority of these studies on emotional obstacles in learning have been based exclusively on observations of children in prolonged treatment. That is to say, children who have been seen once or twice a week for several months or years by a therapist have provided the broad data for generating theories as to what is emotionally specific to learning difficulties. There is not the slightest doubt that we have learned much of value from these studies, and that there is a decided advantage in observing the child over a long period of

---

* All notes appear at the end of the book. See pages 197-199.

time. However, there is serious doubt whether these treated children are truly representative of all children with learning difficulties. Of the 100 non-learners in this study, only 22 were seen in prolonged treatment, but these boys and their families were not representative of the entire group. As we shall see in the final chapter, this small group had special characteristics which made it co-operative toward the idea of prolonged treatment. Thus, the study of the diagnostic records of 100 boys may give a more truly representative picture of the common types of learning difficulties.

We have said that this book is organized around the reasons for learning problems and that the reasons may be many. Nonetheless, all the reasons offered center around the home. Though teachers are undoubtedly sometimes at fault, we have no data with which to make this point. And in the home, most of the reasons for failure in learning *and* success in learning will concern the mother, who is the principal homemaker and the first educator of the boy. It is not simply that we have more information on the mothers than on the fathers; more important, it is that the evidence points to the significant role of the mother, especially in primary grade learning. To be sure, no boy can comfortably succeed in learning if he is confronted with a weak, jealous, or tyrannical father. But such a father does not appear to create as much havoc with the boy's learning as does a similar mother.

With this prospectus, we invite the reader's attention to boys with learning difficulties. For many of them, it soon may be later than one thinks. As Plato said in the *Republic*, "Solon was under a delusion when he said that a man when he grows old may learn many things—for he can no more learn much than he can run much; youth is the time for any extraordinary toil."[2]

Part One

FACTORS THAT

AFFECT LEARNING

ii

*I*T HAS been said that the best method of insuring a long life is to select parents and grandparents who were long-lived. The same may be said of education. The best assurance a boy may have of being properly equipped and motivated to get the most from our educational system is the possession of parents and grandparents of a socio-economic group which places a high value on education. The physical heredity which promotes longevity corresponds to the social heredity which promotes interest in being educated. The fact that one cannot preselect one's physical or social heredity introduces a natural inequality among free and equal men—an inequality which, in the area of learning, requires understanding and remedy.

Differences in social class proved to be one of the few general factors distinguishing the entire learner group from the entire non-learner group. Taking occupation and education of the father as the prime indicator of social class, we found among the 100 learners a much greater proportion of boys whose fathers had "professional" occupations (teachers, ministers, physicians, lawyers, scientists, etc.) or who had some college education. In contrast, among the 100 non-learners, there was a greater frequency of boys whose fathers had occupations which could be categorized as "semiskilled" or who had not finished high school. The percentage of fathers who were skilled craftsmen or had a high school education was about the same for the learners and the non-learners. (See Tables I and II, p. 186.)

Before proceeding further, we must emphasize that a boy coming from an upper-middle-class family is not guaranteed freedom from learning difficulty. Similarly, lower-class origins do not inevitably coincide with a learning problem. These results merely indicate that, all other things being equal, the upper-middle-class boy has a better chance of avoiding a learning difficulty than does the lower-class boy.

Specific Learning Problems, Lower-Class Boys

What, we may ask, are the learning symptoms most often reported by the school about lower-class boys? Three statements are characteristic: (1) low average intelligence; (2) working up to intellectual capacity; (3) has repeated at least one grade. These characteristics may stand out more prominently if we tell what was *not* frequently mentioned by the school. The latter include daydreaming, not working up to capacity, and having a reading problem.

The picture of lower-class boys that emerges from these three characteristics and from reading all of the case histories is one of children whose habits, experiences, and social motivations have kept them from ever having fully exercised their intellects. It is definitely not a picture of boys whose neurotic or emotional conflicts block the constructive use of an easily observable keen intellect.

Case Histories.—These characteristics are well illustrated in the case of Anthony, a lower-class non-learner. By way of contrast, we shall study the case of Raymond, an upper-middle-class boy in the learner group.

Anthony is an eight-year-old who has repeated two grades and is now having difficulty with all his subjects. Although he occasionally disturbs other children with his restlessness, the teacher does not consider him to be a behavior problem. In his relationship to her, he is submissive and co-operative. A group test given by the school and an individual Stanford-Binet Test given by the Institute for Juvenile Research placed him in the low-average range (92 on the group test and 95 on the Stanford-Binet). The psychologist who administered the Stanford-Binet gave as her impression, "The test results give a reliable estimate of his intellectual functioning. He did better on the performance items than on the verbal items."

Anthony is the third of four children, having a younger sister, an older brother, and an older sister. The children are spaced about two years apart. The family lives in a flat having three bedrooms and one bath. Anthony's father is a machinist by trade, has had the same job for six years and earns about $110 a week. The father had six brothers and sisters, finished the eighth grade at fourteen, and then went to work. Anthony's mother also came from a large family in which she was the oldest daughter. She reached seventh grade at the age of sixteen, but then stopped school to stay at home. Her mother was ill from a leg infection following childbirth, and Anthony's mother had to look after her and some of the younger children.

Of Anthony's brothers and sisters, the oldest, Alice, is twelve and in the seventh grade; she is a mediocre student; Frank, who is ten, has repeated the second grade and is now in the lower group of the third grade. Sonia, two, is slow in developing.

The mother works as a mother's helper outside the home four afternoons a week, and on the other days she keeps three neighborhood children in the home. She depends on Alice to help take care of her own children. She describes her husband as a man who is usually pleasant, who does his work and sometimes lends her a hand. Their favorite diversions are television and occasional family get-togethers.

The social worker's impression of Anthony's mother was as follows:

Mother is a short, stocky person who appeared dull, phlegmatic, and uninterested in the examination. She stated that she came at the instigation of the school. She believes that Anthony's chief problem is that he is slow in developing and the school expects him to be normal. If they would place him in a special class and give him individual help with his school work, he would achieve more. Mother states that Anthony's brother repeated a grade and that many children do this. She emphasized again that there was no problem, since Anthony is like all the other children. Her own brother was backward in school. She even feels that there is no problem in school —only the teacher and the school doctor feel that there is a problem.

Anthony's case illustrates the general atmosphere of a lower-class family and its effects on learning. In this environment, the intellectual level is obviously low, and both mother and father are absorbed in the tasks of existence. Not only is little value put on education, but the mother would lose her helpers if the children became interested in school. Pressure, then, is exerted against becoming educated. The results in Anthony are low-average intelligence and grade repetition—repercussions quite familiar and non-threatening to the mother. (Other influences operating here will be commented on in a later connection.)

Raymond is also an eight-year-old. He was not referred to the clinic because of school difficulties, but because of "nightmares, nervousness, biting his nails for the past six months; he also has a strong fear of death, although there has been no death in the family; he is shy and cries easily."

The school report indicates that the school not only considers that Raymond has no difficulty with learning but also that it sees no manifestation of any emotional disturbance. The report says:

No problem. Score of 133 on primary mental abilities test. Very good in reading, arithmetic, science, spelling. Average in writing. He is working to capacity and has a tendency to be somewhat overly serious. Raymond mixes well with the other children and is co-operative with the teacher. This boy seems perfectly normal to me. He is always nicely dressed, acts as our recess play leader, and contributes a good deal to our class discussions. He brought in his collection of rocks, and told about bowling with his father and brother.

Raymond has one younger brother, Ricky, who is five and who is doing well in kindergarten. They share a bedroom in an apartment in an upper-middle-class neighborhood. The mother, who studied undergraduate social work at college, has never worked. Father, who also went to college, is a partner with his father-in-law in a wholesale drug company. The parents are both third generation Americans and belong to the Unitarian Church. Their diversions include reading and going to lectures, plays, and concerts.

The following is pertinent regarding the family's attitude toward school. Mother was concerned about Raymond's first-grade teacher whom she characterized as "unfit to teach." When Raymond brought home his first report card, both mother and father were disappointed that his grades were all fair or average but not excellent. However, they made no issue of it and told Raymond he had done well. Later, at a PTA meeting, Raymond's mother learned from the school psychologist that he was a very bright boy, so thereafter the mother could not tolerate mediocre grades. Later, Raymond came home from school crying because, when he made a reading error, the teacher had said, "Your mother thinks you are a mental giant."

In the case of Raymond, the heightened intellectual atmosphere of this upper-middle-class family is easily apparent. Education is certainly valued, and there are definite indications that it is overvalued. Whereas Anthony's mother can take his grade repetition without a qualm, Raymond's mother winces markedly when her son receives only average grades. Whereas Anthony's mother has a chronic disaffection for the educational system, Raymond's mother likes the teachers who confirm her high opinion and expectations of her son, and dislikes the teachers who have the affrontery to suggest that her son is not a "mental giant." It is quite likely that Raymond's nervous symptoms arise out of the high expectations of him. At present, they do not impinge on his learning ability.

Attitudes toward Education.—Let us now inquire more systematically into the effects of lower-class origin. First, we must call attention to the fact that our findings are much in keeping with the findings of leading educators and sociologists. They have emphasized that each socio-economic class—from lower-lower to upper-upper (in Lloyd Warner's terms)—views and values education in a somewhat different way. The middle-class, most important numerically, values education more highly than does the lower-class, the second largest group. It is not surprising that members of the middle-classes, as professional or college educated persons, highly skilled craftsmen, etc., should more frequently give their children a valued concept of education than would members of the lower-class, such as semiskilled workmen and persons with only a grade school education.

Allison Davis, Robert Havighurst, and James Brossard, among others, have been leading investigators of this problem.[3] All agree that middle-class parents place a premium on education because it constitutes a way for the children to rise in the world economically, socially, and professionally. This is not true, however, of the lower-class parents. Not only have they not had firsthand experience with the advantages of education, but they are likely to view anyone who has risen through education with jealous suspicion. Bossard tells of the emotional reaction of the lower-class father whose son had used the word "preference." He said, "Preference, preference, I'll preference you. You with the fancy words. You can't high-hat me as long as I pay the bills."[4]

The middle-class boy, then, would be likely to win the approval of his parents by doing well in school; whereas, a lower-class boy might lose approval in so doing. However, not only the approval of the parents is at stake. Davis and Brossard and Havighurst, separately have indicated that the public school itself is primarily a middle-class institution. The values it emphasizes are middle-class, and the teachers themselves are drawn from this class. The middle-class boy, therefore, has a chance of winning the approval of the middle-class teacher so long as he adheres to his ingrained middle-class attitudes. The lower-class boy has less chance of winning the teacher's approval because she tends not to understand that her values are different from his and to be exasperated with the lower-class boy who is resentful of demands that he learn. Davis and Havighurst say that the teachers, instead of changing teaching methods to accommodate the differences in attitudes which arise from different social class origins, tend more often to increase the pressure on lower-class children by forcing them to comply with existing methods and values. As a result, many children become frustrated and discouraged with school, and are likely to develop problems in learning.[5]

Development of the Intellect.—We should like to go deeper into this matter because we believe an additional factor is working here. It is true that if a child learns because of external rewards, the reward of approval by parent and teacher will constitute an incentive for learning. But a child cannot respond by learning—no matter how attractive the incentive—unless he is equipped to respond. In this respect, we believe that the lower-class boy is at a comparative disadvantage. *His intellectual apparatus has not been exercised.* In order to converse with a parent or other members of his social class, a lower-class child must rise to the level of the discourse. If the discourse requires only a low intellectual level, the child, out of habit and inertia, finds it a needless expenditure of intellectual energy to rise higher.

Interviews with lower-class parents yield the impression that conversing with them would neither stimulate nor exercise the intellect. They are more preoccupied with the "What is it?" and "How can I use it?" aspects of human existence than with the "Why is it?" aspects. The brute necessities of economic survival compel them to be basically practical—not to wonder about the meaning and the interrelatedness of life. When their preschool son goes through the phase of "Why is this?" and "Why is that?" the parents usually do not know how to respond. Often, perhaps, they react impatiently saying, "Never mind 'Why this is?' It is just that way." The son realizes that it does not pay to communicate on this level.

The intellectual powers of most lower-class boys, then, have never been adequately stimulated. To employ a medical term, these powers have been atrophied through disuse. This may account in part for the lower scores that the lower-class boys in our sample received on intelligence tests. Their scores were most frequently in the 90 to 105 range; whereas the scores of middle-class boys were usually above 105. While intelligence tests strive to measure intellectual ability, it is well known that their scores can be raised by stimulation. Children from orphanages who have had minimal discourse with adults have added ten points to their I.Q.'s after placement in foster or adoptive homes where they communicate more frequently with adults. Similarly, it is known that northern Negroes who are exposed to and stimulated by urban middle-class surroundings, score higher on I.Q. tests than do southern Negroes.

Grade Repetition.—The increased frequency of grade repetition among lower-class boys would seem to stem from the lower value that lower-class parents place on education. The reasons that a child repeats a grade are complex. Ordinarily, one would think that the basic reason is that the teacher believes the child would be helped to master certain subjects if he worked on them a second time. However, there is apparently a big step between considering a grade repetition and actually carrying out the procedure. Sometimes an official educational policy that no child should ever fail intrudes itself. More often, however, the intervention of a parent may decide the matter.

A middle-class parent usually becomes quite concerned if the teacher suggests that his or her child repeat a grade. The mother will visit the school, protest that grade repetition would hurt the boy's self-esteem, and promise that the parents will work with the boy in improving his schoolwork. The teacher, impressed with the sincerity, motivation, and anxiety of the mother, will frequently reconsider the step.

This type of intervention occurs much less often with parents of lower-class boys. More frequently, the teacher is more concerned about the boy's poor school work than are his parents. They will visit the school only after repeated requests, and then will show little motivation to improve the situation. Confronted by such an attitude, the teacher is much more likely to carry out the recommendation of grade repetition. In summary, middle-class parents, for good or bad reasons, tend to care whether their son passes or fails; whereas lower-class parents tend not to care.

Two factors in addition to the father's occupation which are related to socio-economic class showed the same effects on the learning process. These factors are (1) whether or not the mother is employed outside the home, and (2) the number of children in the family. Because they are only in part socio-economic factors, and because they will be dealt with later in another connection, we shall dwell on them now to only a limited extent.

Employment of the Mother
Outside the Home

The economic reasons given by the mothers who worked outside the home were of two kinds. Lower-class mothers frequently stressed that they worked to keep up an existing standard of living—to make ends meet. The father was not making enough money and the mother had to supplement the family income. Lower-middle-class mothers said that they worked to improve their standards of living; their most frequent concrete goal was to save up enough money for down-payment on a house. (The psychological reasons that mothers work will be discussed in the next chapter.)

It is interesting that the working mothers factor had a similar effect on both the non-learner and learner groups. *In both groups, low-average intelligence test scores (90-105) were more frequently found for boys whose mothers worked than for those whose mothers did not work.* One possible reason for this effect was mentioned previously; namely, that the absence of the mother from the home lessens the child-adult intercommunication and that this, in turn, lessens the stimulation of the child's intellect. Furthermore, the child who is thrown on his own uses his learning energy for practical survival purposes rather than for abstract education which may or may not pay off in the dim future.

The Number of Children in the Family

The other factor—the number of children in the family—also has partial socio-economic determinants. Parents may have four, five, or more children for a number of reasons. Sometimes it is a reflection of the fashion or mood of the times. At present, it has been noted that larger families are beginning again to become more frequent in all socio-economic classes. Usually, however, large families are more often found in the lower socio-economic classes. Upper-middle-class parents tend to limit their children to the number they can comfortably afford to educate to a college level. Lower-class parents do not usually consider such factors in determining family size.

Again, the effect of a large number of children was seen primarily in the manifestation of low-average inteligence scores (90-105). *In both groups* (learner and non-learner), higher intelligence scores were more frequently found among children without siblings and boys who had one or two siblings. The lower intelligence scores were more often seen in boys who had three or more siblings. (See Table III, page 187.)

Large family number was seen to have a similar effect in two separate studies by the present author. In one, the relationship of I.Q. scores to number of children in the family was investigated using roughly 2,000 boys and 700 girls who were admitted to the Institute for Juvenile Research. With both boys and girls, the lower intelligence scores (mental defective to average) were more prevalent in families of more than three children; while higher intelligence scores (average to superior) were more common for children of families of one to three children. (See Table IV, page 187.)

In the other study, 550 male neuropsychotic patients in military hospitals were investigated for the relationship between how far they went in the educational system and the number of their siblings. An inverse relationship was found—the more siblings they had, the sooner they stopped school. (See Table V, page 187.)

No doubt there are many reasons for school-leaving. A. B. Hollingshead believes that the lower-class boy leaves school early because he is treated less well by the school system than is the middle- or upper-class boy. "He is made to feel unwanted in the classroom, in the playgroup, in the clubs and in other extracurricular activities that are usually a part of the school situation."[6] Emil Heintz draws attention to the same point and emphasizes that lower-class boys have strong desires to leave school and go to work.[7]

Here, then, we have another factor—large families—which is associated with low average intelligence and leaving school early. This may be due to the reasons mentioned by Hollingshead and Heintz, but it may also result from the particular impact of this factor on the learning process. Just as the absence from the home of a mother who works may diminish the quantity of intellectually stimulating adult-child communication, so may the distribution of the mother's energies among many children cut down on the amount any one child receives.

Ethnic Attitudes toward Learning

Last to be mentioned is a factor which, while not strictly socio-economic, is better described under this heading than any other. It is related to ethnic attitudes toward learning. Certain ethnic groups emphasize the value of learning regardless of the social class of the particular family. In our study, this was seen in reference to Jewish boys. There were fewer Jewish boys in the non-learner group than in the learner group; intelligence scores were higher and grade repetition was rare. (See Tables VI and VII, page 188.) It is well known that Jewish parents, following their tradition of being the people of the Book, value learning not only as a means of coping with and advancing in the external world, but also as a thing in itself. Within the Jewish family, intellectual failure carries with it certain penalties; love of learning brings great rewards. While this emphasis may have unfavorable reverberations in other areas of learning performance, it does not usually reflect itself in low-average intelligence scores or in grade repetition.

Summary

In this chapter, we have strictly limited ourselves to the influence of socio-economic status and allied factors. Supporting the work of other investigators, our study indicates that the influence of class is not negligible. In summary, lower-class origination is associated with low-average intelligence test scores and the repetition of grades. Moreover, if large families are indeed an indicator of lower-class status, this situation also results in the early leaving of the educational system. The reasons for this relationship are considered to be that lower-class parents place a lesser value on formal education and provide less intellectual stimulation because their time and interest are taken up principally with the problems of practical existence.

Can we say that these factors cause emotional disturbance in lower-class boys? If the definition of emotional disturbance is stretched to include any psychic factor which impinges on the learning process, we might say that. However, if the term is reserved for situations of inner conflict, we would probably do better to refrain from considering socio-economic factors under this heading. The lower-class boy is not so much conflicted within himself as he is in conflict with external middle-class values and goals. Moreover, it may be incorrect to say that he has been understimulated intellectually within his family. While from a middle-class viewpoint, he has not received enough stimulation; from a lower-class viewpoint, he has been adequately stimulated. From the latter standpoint, he has been prepared to cope with the usual exigencies of life.

Because socio-economic factors in themselves are not usually considered to be constituents of inner conflict, we shall, with this chapter, conclude our main discussion of them. They have been mentioned because they *are* important and because no discussion of learning difficulties would be complete without reference to them. In the next chapter, we shall take up factors more usually thought of as leading to emotional disturbances—namely, those issuing from family disorganization.

iii

FAMILY

DISORGANIZATION

*i*T IS DIFFICULT to determine which is more upsetting for a young boy—chronic arguments between his father and mother, or a mother who is unavailable because she is employed outside of the home. However, when both these elements are present in the home, one can be sure that the effect on the boy is highly disturbing. Such family disorganization—regardless of social class—could only result in the boy's having chronic uncertainty about whether his home would stay intact and about whether he could depend on his mother.

In our study, we found these disturbances to have a crucial impact on learning. One factor differentiating the non-learners from the learners was the number of *younger* non-learners who had been exposed to severe family disorganization. That is to say, in boys under ten, the percentage of non-learners coming from homes where *both* marital discord and a working mother—*double disorganization*—were present, was almost three times the percentage of young learners coming from such homes.

We may ask what symptoms of learning difficulties are associated with family disorganization. We shall find a picture somewhat different from that of the lower-class non-learner. The evidence suggested that lower socio-economic status affected the boy's motivation to learn. With family disorganization, however, influences impinge on the actual thinking processes. In other words, regardless of basic motivation, the inner anxious turmoil aroused in the non-learning boy by family disorganization appears to take up energy which could have been used for learning.

The characteristic statements made about younger non-learners coming from such homes were: (1) he has thinking difficulties (daydreaming, inattentiveness, and difficulty in concentrating); (2) he is not working up to capacity; (3) he has repeated a grade; (4) he has reading problems. Except for grade repetition, these symptoms are different from the characteristics noted in the previous chapter. (See Tables VIII, IX, pages 188, 189.)

The extent to which family disorganization can cripple a boy's learning capacity may be seen in the case of Leon, a seven-and-a-half year old non-learner. Of him the teacher reports as follows:

Leon is in grade 1A, having been in 1B for three semesters. He is indifferent, dominates other children, is shy, has no sense of responsibility, plays with toys and gadgets, doesn't complete his work, has poor ability to concentrate, will not conform to rules or directions —a very poor student. He is failing all subjects and has special difficulty with reading. He is not working up to his mental capacity. He needs remedial reading and constant help to complete any work at all. At times, he constantly demands attention; at other times, he is in a world all by himself, playing with toys from home. He shows no emotion when reprimanded—not even peevishness. He needs to be prodded and encouraged and made to realize that every lesson is important and that he is a responsible part of the class.

Leon's teacher suspects that the home is at fault, for she writes, "Mother works. When I questioned her about leaving Leon alone at night, she denied it."

This description refers, of course, to a younger *non-learner*. But even in the young *learner* group, the pernicious effects of double family disorganization can be seen to some extent. Here and there even in this group, the school reports indicate symptoms of thinking difficulties and of not working up to full intellectual capacity. Among the young learners who were exposed to double family disorganization, we found an undue proportion of reported inattention, difficulty in concentrating, and daydreaming. This trend tends to confirm our suspicion that the combination of a working mother and marital discord is a highly potent factor interfering with the learning processes in younger boys.

Marital Discord and Maternal Rejection
of the Homemaker Role

Plentiful evidence indicates that marital discord alone is prominently associated with thinking disorders in the son, disorders which lessen the full utilization of his intellectual capacity. While this applies particularly to younger boys, it is true to a lesser extent of the older boys (ten to sixteen). Additional evidence is gained from the notes of the Institute's psychologists about the behavior of the boys to whom they gave intelligence tests. In both the learner and non-learner groups, distractibility was noted more frequently in boys who had incompatible parents than in those whose parents were compatible. The boys with incompatible parents had trouble keeping their minds on the test. In a previously published study on normal eight- and nine-year-old boys *and* girls, this author pointed out this particular effect of parental conflict.[8] Those normal children coming from homes in which parents disagreed about the disciplining of the children more frequently were described by the school as "not working up to full intellectual capacity" than were normal children whose parents agreed about discipline.

Regarding working mothers, in the previous chapter we mentioned only the *economic* reasons given by mothers for their working outside the home, e.g., the desire to supplement the husband's income to meet necessary expenses and to improve the standard of living. We gained little insight into the *psychological* reasons for the mothers' working. While economic reasons might help us to understand why economically deprived mothers work, the psychological reasons might enable us to know why *any* mother works—regardless of her class.

The dominant impression gained from investigating psychological reasons for working by mothers is that the *mother's need to work outside the home represents some dissatisfaction or discomfort in her principal role as homemaker.* The basis for this impression may be seen more clearly in some case excerpts. In these, the relation between the mother's working and marital discord will also be indicated.

Lower-Class Working Mothers.—The first three excerpts are taken from interviews of lower-class mothers. Although they would seem to have sufficient and plausible economic reasons for working, the psychological reasons they give cannot be overlooked.

Mrs. B. is the mother of Tom, a seven-year-old non-learner who daydreams during the class period, has difficulty in reading, and is repeating the first grade. She has been working on a night shift at a factory from 11:00 P.M. to 8:00 A.M. for the past four years. She says she works at night so she can be home during the day to care for Tom and his ten-year-old brother. She reports that she works to pay for her husband's medical bills, and, secondarily, she acknowledges that she likes her job. Tom's father is a cab driver who works on the day shift and looks after the children at night. According to the mother, he goes from clinic to clinic, doctor to doctor, trying to get relief from minor symptoms, thereby accumulating large medical bills.

In general, Mrs. B. impresses one as an adequate wife and mother. She accepts her happy-go-lucky son, and believes he will outgrow his reading difficulty. She complains only mildly about her husband—with reference to his impatient nervousness and hypochondriasis. The compatibility of their marriage is due, in her eyes, to the fact that she is a patient person who avoids argument. Thus, she takes a silent role with her husband, ignoring or humoring him.

A much different picture is given by Tom's father. From his point of view, there is considerable marital discord. He sees himself as the agitated, interested partner, and his wife as the indifferent one. He engaged in a tirade against his wife, declaring that he is doing his and her work while she is just enjoying life. From the social worker's notes:

The father says he does all the housework, cleans the walls, the rugs, and the furniture. She never compliments him on the work he has done. He complains that when she does do the housework, she never cleans under the furniture, so he has to do it himself. She has no interest in the children—only he has an interest. He is the one who sits with the boy at night and helps him with his lessons. He is the one who bought a piano for the older brother to practice on. Several times, when she came home from work intoxicated, sometimes escorted by other men, he almost sought a divorce or kicked her out. When the matter of divorce was brought up, the older boy said he would go with father, while Tom, the younger one, began to cry, quoting the Bible that parents should stay together.

When mother was interviewed a second time and was told of father's version of the marriage, she admitted that much of what he said was true. Her husband, she said, is a good father to the boys. He plays with them and takes them places. She said that originally she worked to supplement the income, but then began to enjoy it and does not want to stop now. Her husband was such a stay-at-home, she said, that she never got a chance to go out and have a good time. Her getting out of the house now that she works gives her an opportunity to have fun with her female and male co-workers.

Why did Tom's mother reject her role as homemaker? She did not simply force her husband to take over her role, and he, out of his own passive feminine inclinations, did not simply force her to give up her true role. The mother's background yields some clues. The maternal grandmother was constantly sick during mother's childhood. She had a nervous breakdown when mother was a small child and could not care for herself or her home, so that Tom's mother gradually took over the responsibility of caring for her neurotic or psychotic parent. Because of these home conditions, she could not go to high school and worked as a waitress until, at the age of twenty, she married Tom's father who was the first man she had dated. It is apparent from mother's background that she was little prepared to take on the role of homemaker. Not only had she not been mothered, but she had had to mother her own mother. Inwardly resentful of this, she later avoided confining responsibility and married a man who would mother her.

Our second lower-class non-learner is Bernard. His mother is a small, thin, poorly dressed and harassed-looking woman. She works from 5:30 P.M. to 2:00 A.M. because the family needs the money, and they are trying to keep the children in Catholic school. She complained about her husband who is seldom home. He works as a janitor for many buildings and generally works from three in the afternoon until the following morning, as well as on Saturdays and Sundays.

Bernard's mother's background reveals the same lack of mothering as does Tom's mother's, but Bernard's mother had not had to mother her own mother. The maternal grandmother died when Bernard's mother was one year old. The grandfather immediately joined the Navy, and she never saw him. Bernard's mother then lived with the families of various relatives. In one family, she was treated abusively and brutally by an uncle who often whipped her. As a result of this treatment, she was too nervous to learn in school, hated it, and went only as far as the third grade. She recalls being unable to concentrate in school because she was always thinking of what she might have done to get a whipping or a scolding, or to be sent away from her current home. When she was thirteen, the humane society arranged for her placement in a foster home. In Bernard's mother's case also, then, discomfort in the homemaker role appears to issue from her lack of readiness and her early emotional deprivation.

The third case is that of seven-and-a-half-year-old Leon. The distinctive feature of this case is that the homemaker role has been delegated to Leon himself. Leon's father is not in the picture, since the parents were divorced three years previously. Mother's marital difficulties are further evidenced by the fact that this was her second divorce. The following notes from the social worker's interview vividly describe the mother's attitude and role:

Mother is an attractive, somewhat overdressed and disheveled woman. She is intelligent and has thought about the problem, yet she demonstrates no particular anxiety about Leon; in fact, much of her anxiety is about herself. About his problem she says, "I cannot understand why he is so rowdy and belligerent in school, because at home I have seen model behavior. With me, he is quite bright; but at school, they tell me, he is restless, inattentive, and cannot concentrate. I've trained him to be quite independent and self-reliant. I work from 6:00 A.M. to 3:00 P.M. in a restaurant in order to provide money for Leon and myself." Therefore, Leon works on his own, prepares his own breakfast, makes his own bed, straightens the home, puts the dishes to soak, and double-checks the house to see if it is neat, wears the clothes he himself has selected from his drawer, picks up the lunch he has made for himself, and goes to school. Also, he is very helpful and likes to do things for the mother. He often vacuums a rug for her. When she is ill, he brings her juices to drink. One night when she fell asleep while waiting for her date, he covered her with a blanket. Mother says that she has worked continually since Leon was six months old, relying on relatives and day homes to take care of the boy.

Regarding Leon's mother's background, she was quite close to her father and was his pet. She did not feel close to her mother, whom she said "never worried about me when I went out at night." When Leon's mother was seven, her three-year-old sister died. She told her mother to have another child, and her younger brother was born the following year. "My mother said I was the one who wanted him, while she didn't, so she gave him to me to take care of." Leon's mother told in detail how she reared her brother—dressed, bathed, took care of him, and selected his school. "He was more mine than my mother's." Apart from this required mothering of her brother, she says her behavior was tomboyish. She tells of fighting, playing ball, of being uninterested in toys or dolls. She bossed the boys and tried to be a leader. "I always wanted to be on equal basis with the boys. The only feminine thing I liked was taking care of my brother."

Leon's mother is not simply unready for the feminine role of homemaker. In simple terms, Leon's mother developed a preference for the male role, enjoying not only an equality, but a supremacy over men. Her brother, husbands, and son appear to have suffered from her need to dominate and to belittle men, to make them servile and dependent.

Leon's mother did not follow the recommendations of the clinic, and nothing was heard about the boy until two years after our interview. At this time, a newspaper report disclosed that he had been brought to a police station for having slept overnight in a garbage can three miles from his home. His explanation was, "I had no place to go and it was raining."

With relation to social status, the mothers of Tom and Bernard were originally from the lower-class and remained in the lower-class; Leon's mother, on the other hand, began in the middle-class and moved downward to the lower-class. We noted that lower-class working mothers who are incompatible with their husbands were frequently found to be overwhelmed by the responsibilities of homemaking because they had been blatantly emotionally deprived in their own childhoods and because at present their husbands were not energetically adequate enough to give them emotional and practical support.

Middle-Class Working Mothers.—The situation is somewhat different with middle-class working mothers who have marital discord. Here we do not observe such open evidence of early emotional neglect and deprivation—and certainly the economic struggle for existence is not so desperate. Instead, the mothers are aggressively in search of status and recognition; they belittle or despise their more passive husbands not because they believe they are merely less aggressive than other men but because they find their mates inadequate. Because this egoistic need in the mothers is closely related to ambitiousness, the subject of our next chapter, we will limit ourselves here to describing one case of double family disorganization in the middle-class.

Mrs. M. is the mother of Charles, one of the young non-learners. She is described by the social worker as "controlled, severely dressed, and combed." She has been separated from her husband for three months. When asked to describe herself, she says she is a very aggressive person, whereas her husband is extremely passive. Mrs. M. feels she wants everyone else to be the same way she is—that is, aggressive—so she pushes rather hard. Charles is like his father—very passive and quiet. She does not feel her aggressiveness has anything to do with Charles's problem. "He is not affected by my aggressiveness—in fact, he boasts about it to the neighbors. He is always bragging about how well I make drapes." Instead, she holds the father entirely at fault, claiming that he is an alcoholic who "drinks up" all his money. She does admit that he works very regularly, holds a responsible job, and has never missed a day's work because of alcoholism. Mother claims that because he drank up so much money, she had to start working about five or six years ago in order to take care of the many bills; she says she has earned a fairly good living. After this, she began a business of making draperies. She and her husband have been separated a number of times before, but Mrs. M. has finally decided that things are entirely too bad ever to improve; thus she believes that her current separation is probably permanent. Moreover, she declares, her husband has not been a good influence on Charles. He is unable to discipline the boy in any way.

Mr. M. is a somewhat passive, benign individual. Mainly, he said, Charles gets too little attention at home. His mother runs around with a drinking crowd and tries to live too high. For years she has been calling the father at the plant several times a day with minor complaints, and this comes on top of all his other concerns as a maintenance man for two factories. He says that she is constantly pushing him around and throwing up to him the things she buys with the money from her interior decorating. The interior decorator crowd have cocktail parties in the late afternoons or early evenings. His wife has to hurry to finish her various orders for the next day, and this frequently takes her until one or two o'clock in the morning. She wakes up very irritable and is pressed for time during the next several days. During this time, Charles receives very little attention and has to fend for himself. Anything the boy does to interfere with his mother's activity brings either a scolding or a spanking. Mr. M. says his own drinking activities are of a mild nature. What little drinking he does began five or six years ago when the mother began working and depreciating his ability to support the family. This deprecation occurred despite the fact that he has always earned an adequate living ($600 a month).

Which parent's version of the marriage is more objective cannot be definitely determined. However, some evidence indicates that Mr. M.'s version might be somewhat more objective. Some support for this came from the interview with Charles. The only time the boy showed strong emotion during the interview was when he was asked about his father. At this point, tears welled up in his eyes, and he related that his father had bought him a bicycle and put it together for him for his birthday just a week earlier, and that he was very happy about this. Another indication came from Mrs. M.'s background. This is her second marriage. She was married at nineteen, but divorced her husband after two years because she did not like his arrogance. Her present husband had been her boy friend when she was fourteen, but because he was not making much money, she married the other man.

Charles's mother came from a stable middle-class home, the

seventh of eight children. Her parents were devoted to each other and to the children. She was good in school and graduated from high school. She remembers herself as being a snippy child, particularly with relation to her father, who was rather strict. The eighth child, a brother, was favored by her mother, and she recalls much rivalry with him. This evidence suggests that perhaps out of jealousy of the younger brother she has a competitive attitude towards men, strives to outdo and belittle them, with the result that the relationships with her two husbands and with her son have not been satisfactory.

Summary

The foregoing case excerpts illustrate the emotional climate of boys' homes in which there is double family disorganization. If a mother not only enjoys working outside the home, but also has difficulty getting along well with her husband, she is ill-prepared for the function of homemaking. If mature femininity is defined as the capacity to adjust to and to enjoy motherhood and wifehood, these particular mothers would have to be designated as immature in their feminine development. While few mothers—and for that matter few fathers—meet the criteria for ideal maturity, they do not fall short as markedly as the mothers we have described. Most parents have some limitations in their capacities as parents or spouses, but these mothers have deficiencies in both respects.

Why does this double family disorganization, issuing from an emotionally immature mother, so markedly affect the son's learning processes? Why does it produce thinking disturbances which, in turn, produce reading problems and grade repetition? We shall not attempt at this point to seek final answers to these questions. Rather, we shall sketch some preliminary answers now, and, in later chapters, we shall return to the same questions.

The particular working mothers who also experience marital

discord are not only physically absent from their children; they are also emotionally absent. Their emotional investments in their jobs leave little positive emotional surplus for their children. Such physical and emotional absence of the mother frequently has been observed to produce anxiety and uncertainty in the child. Anna Freud and Dorothy Burlingham, for example, have investigated the consequences of separation of the child from the mother during the World War II evacuation from London. Children who were evacuated to the countryside without their mothers showed much more evidence of anxiety than did the children who were evacuated with their mothers.[9] Added to this anxiety is the insecurity children feel about marital discord. The question that preys on the child's mind is whether his parents are going to stay together or not.

Anxious uncertainty, then, is the basic feeling resulting from double family disorganization and is the mood which accompanies the boy to the classroom. Absorption in worries about the home prevents his concentration on his school work. Thus, we see him described as inattentive, having difficulty in concentrating, or daydreaming. For the younger boy, this interference with intellectual application prevents the learning of the very important tool subject of reading. Falling more and more behind in his studies, he has to repeat a grade.

The sequence of events we have described is similar to many which have been written of by other investigators. Helen Robinson, for example, states that the principal cause of psychogenic reading disturbance is a home marked by marital discord.[10] Our study supports her opinions about marital discord, inasmuch as it was associated with thinking difficulties in both the learner and non-learner groups. The present study, however, goes one step further when it indicates that the single influence of marital incompatibility usually must be compounded by the influence of a physically and emotionally absent mother in order to produce marked learning problems.

Our purpose in this chapter has been to view the nature and

general effects of family disorganization. The effects of anxious uncertainty and of thinking difficulties contrast with the effects of lower-class origination which appeared to be a lack of stimulus to learn. In the next chapter, we leave the lower socioeconomic class further behind as we consider a highly distinctive middle-class characteristic: namely, the ambitiousness of mothers and fathers.

iv

PARENTAL AMBITION

a LAND in which birth in a log cabin is traditionally considered to be an aid to becoming president must be considered a land of opportunity for achievement and status change. The competitive struggle for status achievement is most marked in the middle-class, the class that wishes to be distinguished from the lower-class and that is striving for the apparently more secure self-esteem of the upper-class. Fearing the disgrace of being left behind in the status race, many numbers of this class exert ambitious pressure on themselves, their spouses, and their children. This pressure frequently finds its focus in the area of learning—inasmuch as education is the "royal road" to higher status. But, as we shall find, ambition has paradoxical effects. Under its demands that one be *more* "equal" than anyone else, some can rise to dizzying heights in learning; while others self-protectively remain at dismal depths.

We shall be concerned mainly with the mother's ambitiousness. We have already dealt indirectly with the father's ambitious drive when we considered the boy's class origins. We found evidence suggesting that when the father is ambitious for and secures achievement, the son is less likely to have a learning problem. The middle-class boy is rewarded at home for achieving, and he has his father as model for productive achievement. It is difficult to separate the effects of the father's ambitiousness from those of the mother's, for ambitious mothers tend to choose husbands who have had education, are ambitious, and seek upper-middle-class status. Thus, it is not surprising, for example, that we found grade repetition to be associated *rarely* with ambitious mothers and *rarely* with college educated or professional fathers. (See Table XI, page 189.) Such parents do not permit failure by the son.

Unlike the other factors we have considered, maternal ambitiousness alone does not differentiate the learners from the non-learners. Both groups had about the same percentage of ambitious mothers. However, maternal ambition in conjunction with other factors appeared to have a direct bearing on whether the son was a learner or a non-learner.

One of these other factors is the boy's intelligence. The learners with ambitious mothers frequently had very high intelligence test scores (over 130); whereas the non-learners with ambitious mothers more often had low average scores (90-105). (See Table X, page 189.) This finding suggests that ambitious mothers of learners take into consideration the actual intellectual capacity of their sons; whereas the mothers of non-learners do not.

Ambitiousness and Learning Symptoms

We may ask what learning symptoms result from the mother's ambitiousness. The symptom seen among *non-learners* was essentially a resistance to the process of being educated. It was not a resistance to a particular subject such as reading, nor a resistance which affected the thinking processes. Rather, it was a resistance to the person doing the educating—regardless of whether that person was the mother or the teacher. Moreover, it did not take one particular form. Occasionally it manifested itself in open rebellion. More frequently, it took a subtler form, such as procrastination or the doing of some activity other than what the educator was interested in.

Even among the *learner* boys with ambitious mothers, we find some evidence of this symptom. Occasionally the teachers commented, "Probably not working up to full intellectual capacity." (See Table XI, page 189.) This comment may have been prompted by the fact that the intelligence rating was so high that the boy would have had to produce considerably in order to be working up to full capacity. However, it is more likely that the comment "not working up to full capacity," indicates that these learners feel the same resistance previously noted in the non-learner group. This supposition is supported by the fact that other learners who had equally high intelligence ratings but who did not have ambitious mothers were less frequently described as not working up to capacity.

Case Histories

Before we attempt to explain these trends, let us first view maternal ambitiousness in action. The following case excerpts— one from the learner group and two from the non-learner group —will indicate the amount and kind of pressure on the son and his way of coping with it.

Mrs. T. is the mother of James, a twelve-and-a-half-year-old boy in the learner group. He has no apparent learning difficulty and earned an I.Q. of 138 on the Stanford-Binet Intelligence Test. He does above-average work in all his studies, but the school comments that he is not working up to full capacity. He was referred to the clinic because of anxiety attacks, insomnia, and a fear of death. Mrs. T. is quite ambitious for her son and daughter, for her husband, and, in a concealed way, for herself. The pressure she exerts on her family as a result of her ambitiousness is evident in the social worker's notes:

Mother sees herself as the maintainer of balanced relationships in the family. She had James double-promoted by the school when he felt inferior about his younger sister's double promotion. She has been pushing father forward lately, since he was out of the limelight and must have felt rejected at the attention given to the three children. James seems to resent his mother, and he does not want to do what she wants him to do. He says he won't, argues and, if she presses him, begins to scream and run around the house. Muriel, three years younger, also objects, but if mother pushes her to the wall, she will finally "co-operate." Mother says she just worshipped James as a baby; the sun rose and set in him; and she thinks that the father felt extremely shut out during this period. She says that James was an active, responsive baby. She revealed with very little feeling that she would overstimulate him so much that he would vomit. Mrs. T. reveals her own competitiveness for status in saying with obvious pride that James was toilet trained before any of her friends' children. Several years ago, James began taking piano lessons—if not at his own instigation, at least with his acceptance. He and his mother had two years of constant turmoil and scenes about practicing, until finally, when the teacher refused to give him any more lessons, she stopped pushing him. Now his sister is doing famously, but James seems relieved that he no longer has to practice. Mother wonders if treatment at the Institute would not make things worse. Merely coming to the clinic, she thinks, would make him feel different and inferior. Interestingly enough, mother says James's symptoms have subsided in the past few months. She was ill for six months with pneumonia. During this period, she had to let things go and found that the atmosphere around the house improved.

How should we classify James in regard to his learning? As having an actual learning problem, a potential learning problem, or no problem at all? By our criteria, he does not have an actual learning problem, but his educational future is uncertain. He has been caught up in the status race that mother is conducting in her own home. For the most part, he is complying with her ambitions; yet we find danger signals in his resistance to the educative process. These signals may be no more than a passing phase in his development, or they may suggest that he will need a less demanding educational program. Finally, James's resistance may indicate that no matter how favorable his later educational setting may be, he might become increasingly resistant to all educational stimuli. Although we do not know what actually happened to James, we do have some information on other similar young men. This will be the subject of Chapter VII.

As we turn now to the non-learner boys with ambitious mothers, we shall find that when the sons resist them, the mother's ambitious pressure tends to be maximal. Whereas the maternal ambitiousness of James's mother may backfire much later, in the following cases, the backfire is early and obvious.

Mrs. A. is the mother of nine-year-old Larry, one of the non-learners. The family is in the upper-middle-class, and the parents agree with each other about the children. The mother does not work. Larry is an only child. In spite of all this, the mother's ambitiousness with relation to her son has obviously misfired. The school report gives the flavor of his learning difficulty:

Larry is average in spelling, barely passing in reading, arithmetic, and penmanship. He is a "smart Alec" type and wishes to be the center of attention. He will tease and push others in order to focus attention upon himself. He will not take the time to think through a problem or question, and would rather write anything down in order to be finished first. At other times, he will go through phases of dawdling or playing with his pencils.

Some conflicts between compliance and resistance to mother's ambition can be seen here. But the conflict is more apparent than real. Although he usually rushes through his work in order to be finished first, this is simply a caricature of compliance. He accepts one fragment of his mother's wish—to finish first— but he sabotages this by doing his work without thinking. In his less frequent dawdling phase, the resistance is more obvious.

The social worker describes the interview with Mrs. A.:

Mrs. A. is a prim, neat-appearing woman who dresses meticulously and appears younger than her 38 years. Her feeling of inadequacy and her need to appear adequate were apparent from her early statement, "I was a teacher, and they say that teachers make the worst mothers." She wants only that Larry be an "average child," but his school work and reading are definitely below average. She finds this difficult to understand because she has been reading to him since he was six months old, and he seemed to enjoy it until he started school. Mother feels that his kindergarten teacher was nice, but that his first-grade teacher did not do well. For the past year, mother has been tutoring Larry intensively at home, but he is not interested and goes along with the session only because he will be punished if he does not. Mother recognizes that the patient might be spiting her because reading is so important to her, but she cannot carry this insight into practice. She feels completely sympathetic with the boy's present teacher, who told her Larry was driving her crazy by his antics.

He shows only one strong interest at home, but he talks about it at such length that she can't stand it. He is highly interested in electricity—in wires, street lights, and traffic objects. He has batteries all over the house and periodically has fantastically ambitious ideas about what he can do with them.

Mother's need for adequacy is evident in her reasons for having Larry. Although he was a planned child, she wanted him because all her friends were having children. It was the thing to do. She describes her own childhood as placid and happy. She enjoyed school and achievement. She was eager for college training and was successful both academically and in school activities. Mother speaks with real pleasure of her teaching experience, which was in a primary grade, and her ability to go on working after her marriage, despite her family's and husband's initial opposition to it. She says that she did regret giving up her teaching when she gave birth to Larry. She described father as a fine man who is easy to get along with, and thought her marriage was quite satisfactory. Although he did not go to college, he has been quite successful as a department head in a large corporation. She reports that he has a very good relationship with Larry and that perhaps she should be as easy-going as he is. However, she needs to have things done "right now" the way she wants them done.

Mrs. A.'s ambitiousness is somewhat different from Mrs. T.'s. Although both mothers are interested in status and of what people think of them, Mrs. A.'s ambition is more personal and results in more controlling pressure than does Mrs. T.'s. The latter seems to stand on the sidelines or at the goal line, urging her spouse and children to greater accomplishment. Her ambition is gratified in reflected glory. She does not care what form success takes so long as it is achieved. Mrs. A., however, is a tighter, less flexible person. She exerts more pressure relating to when the learning task is to be done and how it is to be done. Increased status seems to protect her against criticism rather than to provide her with pleasurable rewards. Furthermore, she is personally identified with her teaching profession. She believes that her son's failure reflects critically on her adequacy as a teacher. Although she is not actually a working mother, she may function as such. Her absorbing and interrupted interest in teaching creates an emotional mother-child separation similar to that occurring when the mother is actually employed outside the home.

Our third mother, Mrs. B., is the mother of ten-year-old Brian, another non-learner. Whereas Larry's mother, in her compulsive insistence on order and progress, primarily wishes to avoid implications of criticism, Brian's mother's ambitiousness is more flagrant, egoistic, and destructive. Brian's school report is somewhat similar to Larry's. He is failing in all subjects despite seemingly good intelligence. Brian does not accomplish school tasks, dreaming away his school time. His teacher has become discouraged because he responds to none of the usual motivating stimuli, and he falls farther and father behind in his work. In his case, compliance to mother's ambition is minimal; the rebellion and resistance are great.

The social worker's interview with Mrs. B. resulted in the following report:

Mother is carelessly groomed, a fleshy blonde. She needs assistance in order to focus on the problem. She constantly repeats that Brian's problems are her mother-in-law's fault. She says that her son "lives in a world all his own." When she asks him to clear the table, he will say, "OK," and when she returns, nothing has been done; he has been looking out the window. When she hovers over him until he does the task, he does it quickly. She has heard similar reports from the teacher—that he can do a forty-minute assignment in ten minutes when the teacher stands over him every one of the ten minutes. At home, he picks on his younger sister, Susie, who is mother's favorite. He criticizes her baby talk. Most of his play is solitary, and he sometimes spends three hours floating boats in the bathtub. Most of his other play is of the cops and robbers variety, and he draws pictures of women trapped in burning buildings, screaming for help. He loves to be with his father, and they play together with his toy train. He resists going to sleep until his mother has come home from work, and he likes to sleep with his father in the parental double bed. He likes his father's parents very much and sees them twice a week. Mother says about this, "Of course he likes them—they worship the ground he walks on. They loathe me and my daughter. They give him everything."

Mrs. B. is not, however, the ordinary housewife who finds herself in the ordinary situation of having her in-laws like her son better than they do her. As the following material illustrates, this situation has extraordinary status implications for her. Her need for increased status and self-importance is reflected in the fact that her early ambition was to be a doctor. In high school, she decided to become a nurse instead. Upon graduation from high school, she did enter a school of nursing but had to drop out during the second year because of illness. Thereafter, she met and married her husband. When he went overseas, she stayed with her in-laws, who sent her to a laboratory school where she studied medical technology. "They were very good to me at this time," she says, "but I guess I was a temporary replacement for their son."

Brian's mother's need for recognition and status and her jealousy of those in the limelight began even earlier than high school. When she was only seven, her parents were divorced on the basis of her father's alleged philandering. She has not seen him since. She describes her own mother as a very youthful and attractive woman who gave music lessons in the daytime and worked as a night clerk in the evening. A housekeeper took care of her and her younger brother. As a child, the mother felt unloved; she says she was overweight and homely. "I wanted to be a musician, but I couldn't play the accordion as well as my mother could." By the time she was twelve, she had begun taking over the rearing of her younger brother. She did all the cooking, but when her mother's boy friends came around, her mother would push her out of the room and take credit for the meal. Brian's mother felt she was in the way and that she could never compete with her mother, who was very attractive and popular. She also feels that her mother preferred her brother, and recently her mother has acknowledged this.

After the birth of her second child, Brian's mother had a

nervous breakdown, depression, and suicidal thoughts. She put these thoughts into action by turning on the gas and by trying to ram the car into a tree. Later she claimed that her husband was laughing at her, and began yelling and slapping at her son whenever he stared out of the window. Finally she saw a psychiatrist who allegedly supported her conviction that she was "low man on the totem pole."

Brian's mother now feels very bitter toward her husband, although this feeling is not reciprocated by the father. The mother admits that her husband protests "that she wears the pants," and although she says that her husband is too domineering, she acknowledges that she makes most of the decisions. She says that while she is aging, her husband still looks quite youthful and appears much younger than she. She thinks he is too vain about his looks. "I just can't talk to him. Every time I do I end up crying." She also suffers from headaches, rage reactions, tensions, and irregular menses.

On the surface, this mother's status efforts seem not too remarkable. She works part-time as a medical technician in order to have some outlets. She moved to a suburb because the children in the city neighborhood were "vulgar, foul-mouthed, stealers, and smokers." She intervened when Brian was to have been failed this last summer, and after she had him tutored, he was passed into the next grade. But those relatively innocuous efforts seemed, in the light of her entire behavior and history, to reflect deep feelings of inferiority and an overriding jealous ambition.

Resistance to Ambition

The mothers of James, Larry, and Brian and the boys themselves illustrate the main thesis of the chapter—that different qualities and quantities of ambitiousness in mothers appear to determine whether the sons are able to comply with or are forced to resist their mothers' ambitious wishes. If they are able to comply, we may observe brilliantly flourishing intellectual processes, at least as measured by the intelligence tests. But even when sons comply, one sees in them traces of resistiveness, and this quality becomes increasingly apparent in the boys who cannot comply with their ambitious mothers.

Why do some boys resist? Since our data do not offer a clear answer to this, we are forced to conjecture about the reasons. Leading theories related to this problem propose the following: (1) the only way the boy can release the aggressive hostility he feels toward his mother is through a passive resistance. He can punish mother by thwarting her. (2) The boy resists in order to preserve his own autonomy and independence against an obtuse, encroaching, and engulfing mother. (3) The boy resists the educational process because he wants to preserve his pride; he fears being measured and taking the risk of incurring mother's unfavorable reaction.

Fear of Being Measured.—Although we believe each of these motivations plays an important part, either separately or in combination, we would like to dwell briefly on the third motive. A fear of being measured is usually thought of as a fear of being found wanting. When faced with a mother who is consistently and unwisely ambitious for him, who requires him to accomplish so that her status and self-esteem be raised, who is interested in him mainly when he accomplishes, the son does not want to fail or fall short of her expectations. He may accomplish for a while if he possesses excellent intellectual capacities; but as the competition becomes keener, he will tend to avoid those situations that might bring "failure." He might respond by being playful about his learning ability, keeping his teachers and parents guessing about what his exact intellectual capabilities are.

The most difficult and complicated situation occurs among boys who are measured and found to be too *good*—and who then find that their mothers actually do not want of them what they have been pushing toward. Of the mothers we have described, Mrs. T. and Mrs. A. are clear and consistent about what they want of their sons. Mrs. B., however, is an example of a mother who is both ambitious for her boy *and* his rival. She competes with her son and her husband for the attention of her in-laws, and may actually obtain more satisfaction from the failures of her husband and son than from their successes. If they fail, she becomes the important and dominant person in the family, the one who presumably receives the favor of the world. When she helps the boy with his homework, his errors may be an occasion for her inward gloating. Thus, the boy *hears* "be successful" and *senses* "Mother will feel better if I fail." He cannot possibly comply with the mother, and thus he becomes increasingly resistant to the educational process.

Passive Resistance.—Another kind of resistance is rather clearly related to the mother's ambitiousness, and may be reflected in complaints that the boy is excessively slow about doing things at home. The boy dawdles, takes a very long time to do a simple task like washing his hands or putting on his shoes. That this behavior is connected with learning difficulties at school is evidenced by the fact that it was complained of by 28 per cent of the mothers of boys in the non-learner group, and by only 7 per cent of the mothers of boys in the learner group. The non-learner boys who are "slow at home" are not necessarily the ones who have the lowest intelligence ratings, nor are they necessarily the ones whom the teacher finds to be slow, dull, or procrastinating. Thus, we may ask, why do these boys behave as they do at home?

The answer can be explained briefly by the adage, "A watched pot never boils." It is the mothers with the greatest ambitious drive arising out of feelings of personality inferiority who most frequently make this complaint. The mothers of the non-learners can be grouped on the basis of whether they possess two characteristics which indicate feelings of personal inferiority: ambitiousness and employment outside the home. The complaint that the son was slow was least frequent when the mother had

neither of these characteristics, more frequent when mother
had one, and most frequent when she had both. (See Table XII,
page 190.) Time hangs heavily for these ambitiously driven
women; each moment lost is a moment wasted in the race for
approval; even the normally slower tempos of their sons' performances tend to exasperate them.

Maternal Integration of Ambition

It appears, in general, that the mothers of non-learners lack
the ability to integrate their ambitiousness into a larger scheme
and to subordinate it to family goals. The basis for this belief
comes from an investigation of whether or not maternal ambitiousness is destructive to the marriage. Of eleven ambitious,
working mothers of learners, eight reported happy marriages.
Of nineteen ambitious working mothers of non-learners, only
nine reported satisfactory marriages. Thus, mothers of non-learners appeared not to have integrated their personal ambitions with
the family goals. It seems likely that in the mothers of learners,
ambitiousness is direct and simple; whereas in mothers of non-
learners, ambitiousness is coupled with competitiveness with the
male sex.

The above considerations may shed some light on a point
mentioned earlier, which involves the relationship of the ambitiousness of the mother to the intelligence test scores of the sons.
Paradoxically, learner sons of ambitious mothers had high intelligence test scores; non-learner sons of ambitious mothers had
lower scores.

Possibly, ambitious mothers of learner boys pressure their sons
only if the sons are quite bright. This pressure, then, helps and
stimulates the boys' learning. According to this view, the ambitious mothers of non-learner boys fail to take into consideration
the limited intelligence of their sons. They pressure them for
achievement regardless of their abilities. The learner group has

no difficulty with learning because their ambitious mothers stimulate rather than overload their intellectual capacities; whereas the non-learner group has considerable difficulty with learning because their ambitious mothers demand too much from their only average intellectual equipment.

It is also possible that the learner and non-learner boys began life with the same intellectual capacity. The ambitious mothers of the learners may have wholesomely stimulated the original capacity to greater intellectual achievement, while the ambitious mothers of non-learners may have tended to compete with the male sex and to diminish or destroy the original intellectual capacity. Difficulties arise, however, when, in a particular case, one has to decide what the original capacity was and what the environmental influences have done to stimulate or dampen it. For definite solutions to this problem we shall have to depend on current research on the nature of intelligence.

To this point, we have said little about the role of the father. He may be ambitious and successful, ambitious and unsuccessful, or not ambitious. Most threatening to the boy is the situation in which the mother is ambitious for the son, while the father, who has failed to meet his own ambition for himself, is covertly jealous toward and competitive with the son. This situation, however, was rarely seen as part of the family configurations of the younger non-learners and was only occasionally observed in the older non-learners. However, it was often noted in the learners. For some reason, this triangular conflict does not characteristically affect learning in the primary grades or high schools. As we shall observe in a later chapter, it is more frequently a consideration in failure at the college level.

However, with relation to direct ambition for the son, what we have said about mother applies equally well to father. When this ambitiousness is well-tempered and maturely integrated into the parent's personality, it can stimulate and challenge the boy's intellectual capacity. When it is excessive or non-integrated, it misfires easily and obviously. Moreover, we suspect that the intellectual compliance to excessive parental ambitiousness of those boys with superior intelligence may have only the brief glow of a shooting star.

This line of thinking suggests Toynbee's description of the way civilizations meet challenge. After establishing that some adversity, pressure, or challenge is necessary to stimulate any civilization's growth, he adds, "If we increase the severity of the challenge ad infinitum . . . we reach a point beyond which increasing severity produces diminishing results . . . and the possibility of successfully responding to the challenge disappears."[11] Some civilizations have succumbed early to too much adversity. Others, like the Eskimo and Polynesian societies, responded energetically to an excessive challenge, coped with it for a long period of time in a tour de force, and then, exhausted, came to a stage of arrested development.

The parallels we draw between the growth of civilization and the intellectual growth of the boy suggest that we are dealing with a very common and basic ingredient of the human personality. The ambitiousness of the parent and the desires to increase one's mastery, self-esteem, and status constitute challenges to the son. These have the same potentiality for good and evil that challenges to civilizations have. Its ability is similar to that which pertains to atomic energy. Well channeled, it can be a great constructive force; unchanneled, it can be very destructive.

v

BIRTH ORDER

AND PARENTAL

EXPECTATIONS

OF MATURITY

a SUBTLE but powerful influence on the growing boy arises from his position among the children in the family, i.e., from his being the first-born, a middle-born or the last-born. Parents have different maturity expectations of the first-born and the last-born child. Specifically, they generally expect the first-born to be more mature and permit the last-born to be less mature. How these expectations affect learning and other forms of behavior will be the subject of this chapter.

Expectations arising from family position differ from those stemming from parental ambitiousness. Parental ambitiousness looks toward the future and envisages the boy's status some years hence; maturity expectations are geared more to the present. Thus, while the status-conscious parent may wish the son eventually to enter one of the professions, the maturity-conscious parent may wish that he knew how to tie his shoe laces and keep his room in order today. If maturity expectations are in keeping with the child's actual age, wholesome effects will undoubtedly result. But sometimes the expectations are excessively high or low: unwholesome effects generally result if parents expect that a three-year-old boy consistently behave like a six-year-old, or constantly permit a six-year-old to behave like a three-year-old.

The initial and central finding of this part of the study was discovered when we compared the ordinal positions of the learner and non-learner boys. We found little difference in the positions of middle and "only" children, but a striking difference in the percentages of the eldest and youngest. Eldest or first-born boys were found almost twice as frequently in the group *without* learning problems. Conversely, youngest or last-born boys were found almost twice as frequently in the group *with* learning problems. (See Table XIII, page 190.)

Because we had collateral evidence from another source, we were not prepared to dismiss this trend as of accidental significance. We investigated 1,300 boys and 500 girls who came from comparatively small families (two or three children) and who were clinic admissions to the Institute. We found that first-born children were more frequently described by their mothers as being "bright" and more often obtained high-average to superior scores on intelligence tests than did last-born children. The percentage of first-born boys described by their mothers as "bright" was twice that of last-born boys. For boys, there was no difference in intelligence scores. With the girls, although the maternal descriptions of "bright" were equally frequent for first- and last-born youngsters, their descriptions of "slow" were almost two times more frequent for the last-born girls. Furthermore, the first-born girls had a significantly greater percentage of intelligence test scores ranging from high-average to superior, and the last-born girls obtained a significantly greater percentage of scores ranging from dull to mental defective. (See Table XIV, page 190.)

Reasons for Differences
between First- and Last-born Children

Disposed, then, to consider this trend seriously, we thought of three possible reasons to explain it. The first was that the mother may be more tired of child-rearing when she is raising the last-born child and may give him less mothering. We were inclined to discount this possibility because this trend was seen even in small families. In any event, we could find no evidence to prove or disprove this hypothesis.

The second possible reason was that the first-born has a head start in learning achievement, and he strives to maintain this ascendency over his younger siblings. The last-born, being at the bottom of the "pecking order," becomes discouraged with trying to compete with his older sibling and selects an area other than learning as his competitive strength. Although we did see situations like this in some cases, we did not find that sufficient consistent data strongly supported this explanation.

The third possible reason was that the parents have a different emotional relationship with their first child than they do with their last. We were eventually able to find the best supporting evidence for this reason. The first hint that learning differences had to do with maturity expectations came from the previously mentioned investigation of 1,300 boys and 500 girls. It revealed that mothers described their children as "immature," or as "acting babyish," more often when speaking of last-born boys and girls than when describing their first-born children. Looking, then, at our 100 learning boys and our 100 non-learning boys, we found that the teacher's description of boys as "overly serious or sad" was given much more frequently for first-born than for last-born boys. The description "carefree" was more often applied to the last-born.

At this point, we thought the following regarding the psychological situation of the eldest and youngest: The first-born encounter a variety of expectations and stress. The parents, unfamiliar with what children are like, tend to expect them to act like the parents, to be miniature adults. Also, the parents are unsure about their adequacy as parents and measure their competence by how well the first-born thrives. The oldest child, then, has the burden of having to come up to the parents' higher standards of maturity and of maintaining the self-esteem of the parents as parents.

This closeness of the success of the child to the feelings of the parents is further increased by the parents' use of the oldest child as a substitute parent. If the family is under some stress, most often it is the oldest child whom the parents take into their confidence and with whom they share their anxiety. Even when there is no stress, it is more often the oldest who is asked to look after the younger children and to be a proper example for them. Because of these expectations, life, then, tends to be more serious for the eldest or first-born.

In contrast, the youngest is much less likely to have to meet such expectations of responsibility. He is looked after rather than required to look after. The parents tend to be more relaxed in their "do's" and "don't's"—sometimes because they have been too strict with the older children. Thus, the youngest is not as rule-conscious as is the oldest. Moreover, in their relaxation, the parents are more inclined to enjoy the last-born. The oldest child is expected to cope with that half of life concerned with the duties of stern reality. The youngest child is permitted to enjoy that half of life concerned with the pursuit of happiness.

These, then, are the general—though not invariable—considerations which apply to the positions of the eldest and the youngest in the family. Usually the oldest child is the vehicle for the parents' ideas of responsibilities in life, and the youngest is the vehicle for their conceptions of the pleasurable privileges of life. The "grown-up" portion of the parents' personality is more often assigned to the eldest, and the more childlike portion is more often assigned to the youngest.

Evidence supporting this thesis was seen in the family stress coming from the situations in which mothers worked outside the home. This situation calls for the appointment of a parent substitute among the children. We found that among both learner and non-learner boys whose mothers worked, there were many more eldest children who were described by their teachers as "overly serious or sad." The youngest children in both groups were no more frequently overly serious when mother was working than when she was not working. (See Table XV, page 191.)

This trend indicates that the responsible duties fall upon the shoulders of the oldest when the mother goes out to work. That the oldest is more serious suggests that he consciously accepts responsibilities even though they may prove to be too much for him. He puts aside his own life pursuits in order to accommodate the parents' need for help. That the youngest child showed no increase of seriousness suggests that he is much more protected against the increased responsibility, basically does not consider that to be his affair, and leaves the matter to the older siblings.

Using these reflections, we considered again our initial findings that there was an unusual predominance of youngest children in the boys *with* learning problems. We might then explain this by postulating that the youngest child approaches the learning task with much less seriousness and with a much lower expectation of himself than does the oldest child. When an extra bit of effort is needed to persevere through a new step in learning, the youngest child tends less often than the oldest child to find within himself the wherewithal for that extra effort.

Another question which interested us was whether the problems the first-born have in learning are different from those experienced by the last-born. Although the oldest children appeared less likely to have learning problems, they certainly were not immune to them. For our investigation, then, we shall focus on the 33 first-born and the 28 last-born non-learners.

We especially noted a difference between the oldest and youngest in the classroom situation—not in their intelligence test scores, in working up to capacity, in thinking difficulties, nor in proneness to reading difficulties. Rather, the difference was most evident in their resistance reactions to the learning task. The main characteristic of the first-born was a contrariness, an excessive expression of individuality as indicated by the most frequent comment of the teacher, "He resists directions." This sometimes barely disguised "I won't" or "I'll do it my way" of the first-born boys contrasted with a helpless, immature, apparently disorganized, "I can't" frequently characteristic of the last-born youngsters. Thus, the most frequent teacher's comments about the youngest children were: "socially immature," "speaks in an infantile manner," "shows need for affection," "hands in incomplete assignments," "careless."

Learning Problems: First-born Boys

The characteristics of the first-born non-learners may be better seen in the following descriptions of classroom behavior:

1. Bobby, seven years old, is unable to do any directional work. He does not understand abstract conceptions and does only one-third of his written work. He often asks questions with obvious answers. He bothers other children who are working; since he does not follow the directions, he thinks he is finished with his work. He likes stars on his paper, but cannot understand why he does not receive them.

2. Alan, fourteen years old, is a non-conformist. He has frequent outbursts of temper, and is described as "a dual personality" and "very solitary."

3. Jerome, ten years old, appears to be constantly afraid. He never smiles and seems not to mind being punished. His behavior in the classroom is good, but he is perpetually in trouble in the halls. He takes delight in using dirty language, telling dirty poems and stories. He writes them on the blackboard if not watched. He is very abusive to the patrol girls and monitors. The school has tried to reach Jerome in every way possible—through praise and rewards—but with no apparent result. His younger brothers are in school, too. They are daydreamers like Jerry but seem more childlike.

4. Bill, fourteen, is a left-handed boy who stutters at times and has had great trouble learning to write and read. He has strong reversal tendencies and sometimes has been involved in fights. He often uses obscene language. In personal hygiene, he is frequently dirty.

5. James, nine years old, reads and knows simple words one minute but forgets them the next. He was in second grade for two years and was prodded in reading. Reading may have been overemphasized to the point where he now dislikes it. However, he does like books concerning nature, science, etc. He is not a behavior problem at school.

6. Steve, age nine, is unable to read and complete sentences of the third-grade level. He does not remember sounds or words of the first-grade level, and can do nothing by himself except simple addition and subtraction. His younger brother is in the second grade, but is emotionally unstable and cries when he fails to do good work.

In all these examples of first-born boys we can see some variety of resistance to pressures and demands. The resistance may take the form of passive autonomy, as in "being in a world of his own" or "unreachable," or the form of a submissive contrariness, as in reversal of writing, forgetting a word just learned, and asking inane questions; or it may express itself as a more open revolt against rules as in "non-conformity" and "using obscene language." We do not find simple childlike reactions, although here and there the teachers have noted that these are present in the younger siblings.

Learning Problems: Last-born Boys

1. Richard, seven years old, is unable to work alone. He plays all the time, is a careless worker, and often masturbates. Because he speaks in an infantile way, he needs special help in speech correction.

2. Peter, eleven years old, is exceedingly restless and disturbs others in school. He is not making satisfactory educational progress. He is virtually a non-reader at present. Because of his wild, uncontrolled behavior in the schoolroom, he has been transferred from two other schools.

3. Martin, age ten, is a discipline problem. He is immature socially, and frequently brings toys to school. He bothers the other children and is inattentive. He does respond to supervision and encouragement.

4. Edward, nine years old, is retarded in reading ability. He apparently is completely lacking in self-confidence. He exhibits many evidences of need for the affection and approval of adults. He frequently asks to be excused from class to go to the bathroom. He is affectionate toward the teacher, working well with one adult and seeking the approval of that person.

5. John, age seven, is inattentive and careless with supplies. He never completes anything; in fact, he sometimes does not start his task. He is retarded in mastering such personal chores as dressing. Although failure makes no impression on him, he is very happy when praised.

6. Robert, seven years old, is failing in his academic work. He has a speech impediment, involving omission and sound substi-

tution, especially with "l" and "r," and multisyllabic words confuse him.

7. Peter, eight years old, is inattentive in school. His work is done carelessly and incompletely. He lacks the energy necessary to do his work, and when made to complete a task, he becomes sullen. He is quite enthusiastic if he succeeds, but he shows indifference to failure.

8. Kenneth, age nine, has not worked up to his mental age expectancy since the first grade. He has received special individual help, and he apparently tries. The school believes his weak retentive powers are most influential in his continuing failure.

9. Jordan, eleven years old, stole money from his classmates and the teacher. He is aggressive toward children, restless, noisy, and unable to concentrate.

10. James, age eight, is restless and has an attendance problem. He chews pencils and rulers and eats crayolas and paste. Often he crawls on the floor and enjoys sitting under the seat.

11. Donald, nine years old, is socially immature, has a speech problem, and is more interested in what other children are doing than in his own work. He seems to crave affection and is a great idler.

In these examples of last-born boys, one perceives a more immature, loosely organized, plastic personality. In contrast to first-born boys, who may wall themselves off from the educator in order to resist pressuring demands, the last-born children seem to be not only accessible to the teacher, but they actually crave contact with her. They have less need, apparently, to do their schoolwork in their own way. They are childlike and can be led. Moreover, one does not get the impression that the last-born boys have been constricted by rules and are fighting these internalized strictures (as is the case among first-borns). Rather, these examples indicate that they feel a comparative lack of rules, that their impulses are spilling out.

Early Learning and Sibling Position

In continuing our attempt to differentiate the learning difficulties of first-born and last-born boys, we looked next at the reactions of the first-born to early learning situations, those experienced much previous to entering school. Here the educator is the mother, and the learning situation involves feeding and bladder control. We found trends directly parallel to those discovered when the teacher was the educator. First-born boys were especially likely to have had feeding problems; whereas, last-born boys were particularly likely to have had bed-wetting difficulties. (See Table XVI, page 191.)

In regard to the feeding problems of the first-born, we believe that these reflect resistance to pressure. A mother, inexperienced with her first-born and anxious to do well by him, will usually pressure the child to eat; and the child will frequently react to avoid the pressure by refusing to eat or by vomiting. If the mother is tense for additional reasons such as marital discord, her pressure will be an admixture of irritability and punitiveness and will produce more resistance in the child. The boy's later resistance to incorporating new ideas may spring from his earlier resistance to incorporating food.

We believe that the bed-wetting of the last-born reflects the comparative lack of controls placed on the youngest child. As was mentioned before, the last-born child is usually treated more permissively and made less rule-conscious than the first-born. The youngest child's occasional lapses in bladder control are looked upon more indulgently and with less anxiety by the parents. If the mother is emotionally upset and disorganized due to marital discord, the boy may be exposed to an increased bombardment of stimulation and fewer controls—leading to increased disorganization. Later, when he tries to organize himself for the learning tasks in school, he may have insufficient controls over his overflowing impulses—just as earlier he had difficulty controlling his spilling urination impulse.

We are, then, led to believe that there are at least two kinds of learning difficulties. One is the pressure-resisting kind seen most often in first-born boys; the other is the disorganized spilling kind seen most often in last-born boys. Phrased in somewhat more technical language, the first kind of problem constitutes an inner rebellion against the internalized demands of the parents. The second kind constitutes a swamping of the psyche with uncontrolled impulses stimulated by the parents.

We also have evidence linking these characteristics with what happens in the family. This comes from the actual details of family life and, in particular, the mother's personality. As the following examples indicate, the first-born non-learner is sailing on a very taut ship. The social worker's description of his mother is often, "mother is controlling the child"; "mother is punitive with the child when he misbehaves"; "mother is given to intellectualizing instead of feeling"; "mother expects the child to be well-behaved"; "mother is cold"; "mother is reserved." Father, as described by mother, is frequently "punitive to the child" and "expects too much of the child." The undertone of demand and will toward the child—rather than of feeling—is quite obvious.

In contrast, the last-born non-learner seems to be sailing on a chaotic ship, without a rudder, which is in danger of being swamped by the uncontrolled seas. The social worker's description of the mother is often, "mother is obviously depressed"; "mother is worried and anxious"; "mother became tearful during the interview"; "mother is overdressed"; "mother is against forcing the boy"; "mother is closest to this boy, thinks he is lovable." Father, as described by mother, "has beaten me often," "he gambles and drinks." Here, family disorganization and the swamping of the boy by the mother's uncontained impulses are the keynotes.

Mothers of First-born Non-Learners

The following examples will more graphically illustrate these trends:

1. Richard's mother is neat and smartly dressed. She is quite serious. She says that Richard is having social difficulties. He creates disturbances in school and at home. He refuses to do ordinary things. She says: "I tell him to do something and he does just the opposite. If we warn him against it ten times, he will do it anyhow. If we don't warn him, he won't. But I've got to protect him against his own folly. I always hoped to have a near-perfect family life, but I just can't control Richard. . . . When he was five, he wanted to be the baby when he was playing house, but I wouldn't permit it because it is not the healthy way of thinking."

2. Jerry's mother is wearing a tailored suit; she appears very reserved, but occasionally becomes briefly animated. She tends to intellectualize. She was a social worker prior to marriage. She says that when Terry was an infant he could keep very little food down. He often had stomach spasms and spit everything up. The doctors called it "projectile vomiting." People and noises made him nervous. Mother reports that she gave Terry an I.Q. test before he entered school and recently gave a reading-readiness test to a younger child who is in kindergarten.

3. Robert's mother is dressed in a very simple and neat manner. She is quite tense, almost in tears. She says that regardless of what measures they take to punish Robert, such as taking away privileges or reprimanding him, he maintains a composed, controlled manner. He needs punishment principally because he fights with his younger siblings. To mother, this is a severe problem which annoys her because the boy seems so much in control that she can do nothing. He has few friends and is quite content to do things on his own. She has tried to get him into social

groups and has volunteered to be a den mother, but Robert refused. She goes to meetings once a month at the Association for Family Living—purely from intellectual interest. Her husband attends on Fathers' Night, but he is not enthusiastic about it. She admits that she feels guilty about Robert's early life: "I was so overwhelmed by the duties of three children that frequently I did not have time to listen to Robert when he came to me with quesions or complaints." He never had the time to be a baby because his brother was born when he was twenty months, and another sibling thirteen months later. She says she felt overworked during the early years, and that Robert had to grow up quickly.

4. Harold's mother is plainly dressed, rather controlled, and takes an intellectual view of things. She says Harold has an interest in the unusual—such as reading about poisonous and non-poisonous snakes. Earlier, he was interested in outer space and the planets. Moreover, he cannot be led to be interested in the usual things. He asks very "grown-up" questions. Mother says she used to worry about his small appetite and about a positive TB patch test. She tried to force him to eat, and the more she forced, the greater the difficulty became. Finally she gave up, and the feeding problem disappeared. She said her own mother was domineering and would tell her that she must eat all the left-overs.

Mothers of Last-born Non-Learners

1. Peter's mother is quite anxious and overprotective of Peter. We observed her standing close to the patient. When beckoned for an interview, she patted patient on the cheek and straightened his tie. She was extremely apprehensive and sure that Peter was afraid of this place. She says it is difficult for other people to comprehend the patient's ways—only she understands. She says Peter is extremely good-hearted, never asks for much, and

has many positive traits. Father is home very little, frequently going to taverns at night. Even when he is at home, he does not show emotional feeling, and is not very affectionate.

2. Steve's mother is quite ill-at-ease and obviously depressed. She is definitely reaching out for help. She says that her father died when she was two, and that she has always been close to men; she has hoped to find a man like the man she conceived her father to have been. She related tearfully how difficult her life has been, especially since her mother committed suicide by hanging four years ago. Since the suicide, she has had recurrent depressive episodes. She feels sorry for herself, and several times has dreamed that the house was on fire. She has not been able to give Steve much attention. She cannot understand, though, why he seems to act younger than his age, speaks in a juvenile way, and is still enuretic. She is rather satisfied with the scholastic progress of her older son; her only misgiving is that his genitals may be too small.

3. Gary's mother seems overdressed, has bleached hair, and uses makeup extensively. She expresses her feelings in quite a dramatic manner, and seems to have considerable warm feeling for her son. Gary amuses and exasperates her with his gay, elfin, carefree attitude. Mother feels guilty when she has to punish him. He still sucks his thumb at the age of nine. Father and mother are not of the same religion and have never gotten along well. They have had several violent battles in which mother was physically injured so that now she is very much afraid of father. Father has always gone around with other women, especially when mother was pregnant, and brags to mother about his conquests. Mother works as a waitress. Father seriously objects to mother's excessive drinking, but mother says it is not excessive. She does feel that she is always rushing about and is upset most of the time. She and her husband are about to separate, but think that the boy is unaffected by the prospect of this event.

4. Frank's mother is obese and shy and friendly. She shows a great deal of feeling to Frank. She is very ill-at-ease, wringing her

hands almost continuously. Frank is the second of two boys. His older brother is more reserved than he, but Frank is more sociable, makes friends more easily, and is more lovable. The older boy is a very good student and is serious-minded. He and father seem to get along better and have more things in common. Mother is closer to Frank. Although Frank is independent in some ways (he goes for long bike rides with mother's brother), he is infantile in others. She has protected him from getting hurt. Although he is seven, she still feeds and dresses him. He does not obey very well, but mother is not disturbed by this. Although she has to repeat directions four or five times before he does what she asks, she does not find it necessary to punish him severely or to spank him. The only difficulty with her husband is that he drinks. He comes home drunk twice a week. He is never abusive to her or the children, though he often makes promises which he is unable to keep.

Mothers of Oldest and Youngest Non-Leaners:

An Analysis

In these examples we can discover what appears to be a common characteristic of the mothers of first-born non-learners: *an emphasis on order and conformity*. How the child's impulses and feelings are regulated is more important to the mother than the feelings themselves. Mother expects a high degree of self-regulation not only of the first-born but also of herself.

In contrast is the common denominator of the mothers of last-born non-learners, which appears to be an emphasis on *impulse gratification and release*. The child's expression of feeling is more important to the mother than how the feeling is regulated or modulated. Again, mother not only allows emotional gratification in the last-born child, but also permits it in herself.

This contrast may be described in other ways. We may say,

for example, that the mothers of first-born non-learners tend to be compulsive; whereas mothers of last-born non-learners tend to be hysterical. We may also describe mothers of first-born non-learners as tending to use their sons as narcissistic extensions of themselves. They try to use him to avoid shame or other blows to pride. They are often punitive and depreciative if the boys do not measure up by playing a grown-up role. On the other hand, the mothers of last-born non-learners tend to use the boy to requite their needs for affection, sexuality, and infantilism, and to assuage their feelings of guilt. If the sons do not play the little-boy roles cast for them, the mothers often become tearful, distraught, and reproachful.

We have, of course, combined all these characteristics under the rubric of maturity expectations. Thus, excessively high maturity expectations—as seen in the case of the first-born—mean excessive regulation of impulses. Excessively low maturity expectations—as seen in the case of the last-born—mean excessive stimulation of the impulses. The first-born reacts by exhibiting a persistent open or masked resistance to pressure; whereas the last-born reacts with a disorganized, overstimulated emotional outflow. The first-born is caught up in a battle between conforming to and resisting mother's regulatory pressures; whereas the last-born is involved in a conflict between succumbing to and resisting mother's tantalizing overstimulating tendencies.

The pertinence of these reactions to learning is complex, and we will be satisfied if we have provided only some preliminary insights. It appears, though, that two conditions for successful learning are indicated here. One condition is that the boy not reject the incorporation of new ideas, and not regard the educator's efforts as a pressuring infringement of his autonomy. In the first-born non-learners, this condition for learning is comparatively lacking. The other condition is that there be sufficient regulation of the child's excitatory impulses; the environment must be consistent, patterned so that the boy can focus his energies on the learning tasks rather than spilling them randomly.

This learning condition is comparatively lacking in the environments of the last-born non-learners.

These conditions for learning and the lack thereof were noted in a study of normal children and mothers carried out by the author. These children were in the age-range of eight to nine, when intellectual mastery is the prime developmental task. The least well-adjusted of these normal children were of two types: those who were overregulated and feared ingesting new ideas, and those who were overstimulated by a chaotic, primitive family atmosphere.[12]

We have left much unsaid on this subject and have not fully explored many interesting side trails. Because we believe that birth-order repercussions merit serious attention, we have devoted space in Appendix B to a more detailed discussion of these matters. (See pages 176-185.)

AGGRESSION AND

SUBMISSION

*A*GGRESSION and submission are the last factors we will consider in our survey of learners and non-learners. One aspect of this topic is grossly evident and relatively simple to understand. This has to do with the boy's behavior in the classroom. Why are some boys overly aggressive or overly submissive? This question is very important since the hostile, aggressive boys are greater problems to the schoolteacher than are the slow learners. The other aspect of the topic is more complicated and deals with the relation of aggression to intelligence and reading. We shall take up this question after first considering aggression and submission in the classroom.

Behavior which disrupts the schoolroom is naturally troublesome to the teacher. Of its milder forms the teacher often writes: "bothers other children," "makes excessive demands for the teacher's attention," "is stubborn." In its moderate form, the description changes to: "cannot get along with other boys and girls," "defiant to the teacher." Disruptive behavior in its severe form is so extremely troublesome that the boy is expelled or such a step is considered. This behavior was noted in both the non-learners and learners, though to a lesser extent in the latter group. The opposite kind of conduct was also seen in both groups; some boys were submissive and anxious to please.

Parental Projection of Blame

We should like to consider what family influences may account for these kinds of behavior. Our study revealed a probable connection between the boy's behavior and his parents' tendencies to reject or accept responsibility for their faults—that is, their tendencies to belittle or to blame others. To be more specific, in both the learner and non-learner groups, the more the parents were inclined to say, "It's *not* my fault," the more often the son was overly aggressive; and the more often the parents tended to say "It *is* my fault," the more frequently was the son co-operative, submissive, or anxious to please. (See Table XVII, page 192.)

We saw these tendencies of parents most clearly in their reactions to their son's having an emotional problem. As we have said before, parents feel that they are being blamed when their child is referred to a special institute for psychological help. Even before this point has been reached, mother and father frequently accuse each other of being chiefly responsible for their son's problems. When they arrive at the clinic, these mutual accusations may increase. In some families, though, the parents close ranks and make the school the scapegoat. In still other families, one or the other spouse guiltfully accepts more blame than is warranted.

We are interested mainly in the situation in which the parents accuse each other. Not only does this lead to hostile aggression in the son, but it also sheds light on family disorganization. Again, we shall have somewhat more to say about the mother than the father—not because the mother is more likely to be fault-finding than the father, but because her attacks may be more damaging to domestic tranquillity than the father's.

In a marriage, the tendency to blame the spouse can be noted in either mate. What the other spouse can be blamed for is actually either a fault of the blaming spouse or a fault in some-one else with whom the blaming spouse cannot fight. Thus, the husband may lose some money gambling, feel temporarily guilty about his wastefulness, and come home and accuse the wife of spending too much money on food, or even of being a poor manager, a fool, a spendthrift, etc. The same sequence of events could take place if the husband lent his brother some money which the brother spent on a fancy automobile rather than on getting out of debt as he promised. Because he needs to be loyal to his own family, the husband's irritation with his brother may go underground and come out as a reproach to his wife for not being careful enough about money.

The wife may behave in a similar way. She can project her own faults onto her husband. If she has neglected her housework or been away from the children too much, she can upbraid her husband because he takes no interest in the home and is not a real father to the children. Further, if she has been kept quite busy worrying about and looking after a sister who does nothing for herself, she can reproach her husband for his lack of in-dustriousness. It is not surprising, then, that a preponderance of such unfair criticism impinging on human sensitivities should result in hostile aggression. Nor should it be surprising that when such blaming is directed at the son, he often develops attitudes which are so hostile and destructive that he is in danger of being expelled from school.

In what way may mother's finding scapegoats, her blaming others, actually affect the son? First, he learns *by identification* or *imitation* that the best defense is to attack. Whenever he feels guilty about something, he does not solve the guilt by con-trition or reparation or by examining his own behavior. Instead, he finds fault with the school or does something to make the teacher overreact agressively to him. Then he can say to him-self and others, "You see, the teacher *is* mean." A milder example of this tendency is the boy who explains all his fracases with the other boys by saying, "They started it."

Second, if the boy has been his mother's scapegoat, he may be *chronically enraged.* He has had little or no opportunity to discharge his anger against his mother. He does not want to lose his emotional contact with her. She may become cold or violently angry if he counters her unjust criticism with anger. He is, then, left with a mixture of hate for the outside world and hate of self. He goes to school with a reservoir of hate and anger that breaks through as hostile aggressiveness toward his classmates or his teacher.

Third, if the father rather than the boy has been the butt of the mother's vilifications, the son's model for masculine identification is severely damaged, or at least made doubtful. If the boy believes his mother, or if it is dangerous not to believe her, he does not wish to be like his father. If he *is* like his father, he is subject to the same criticism and contempt that father receives. However, when he joins his mother against his father, he feels guilty for deserting father and for not defending him. If, for various reasons, the mother has not invited him to join the anti-father group, the boy has no place to go; he can only be more like father or more like what mother pictures father to be. In this case, the boy over-identifies with the father. His break with mother is intensified by her frequent remarks, "You are just like your father." And if the son is thus given a bad name, he will, in his school behavior, live up to that bad name.

This preamble may make more understandable the trends we have discovered. As we mentioned, *the tendency of the mothers to blame others rather than themselves is highly associated with the sons' exhibiting hostile aggression in the schoolroom in both learner and non-learner groups.* This aggressiveness is most frequent when, in an atmosphere of marital discord, the father is the one that mother blames. However, it also stands out, although less frequently, when there is no marital discord and the school rather than the father is the object of mother's blame. In this latter case, the boy goes to school with the impression that the teacher is mean, unfair, or "dumb." If he gets into trouble at school, he knows his mother will upbraid the school rather than discipline him.

Case Histories

Let us see how this works out in actual cases.

Non-Learners.—Owen is a twelve-year-old in the non-learner group. The school report reads: "Owen is a non-conformist, a dual personality to the n'th degree. He constantly annoys the other children and defies the teacher." Items checked regarding his behavior are: sullen, temper outbursts, selfish, quarrelsome, acts smart, is destructive, teases all the children, excessive demands for teacher's attention, defiant, stubborn, and an attendance problem. Although he has an I.Q. of 126, most of his grades are C's or D's because he fails to complete his assignments.

At present, Owen's school system refuses to accept him as a student in his regular school because of his inability to get along. He remains at home with a visiting teacher and will not be re-accepted until the results of the Institute's examination are provided to the school.

Concerning the mother, the social worker's notes read:

Mrs. G. is a thin, small woman who proved evasive and defensive. At one point, she had to be confronted with the fact that she left out important information. She agreed that she had, and then got off on a long harangue against father while fully absolving herself. Making it clear that "I get along with him," mother told how Owen has had school trouble. She freely blamed the school-teachers and gave examples of their applying too much pressure. She says Owen cannot take pressure. He can do the academic work if given sufficient time. "He is slow," she said. "I can appreciate that. I was the same way." She then blamed father for being too much of a perfectionist. Father demands instant order, obedience, and conformity. "It is hurry up and shut up." He often strikes Owen with little provocation. Her husband is always "tense" and in a hurry. He plays the radio too loudly. He strikes out suddenly if angered. He becomes nervous if mother points out that he is wrong; he says she needs a psychoanalysis. He has a time fetish and brooks no delay. "I wish sometimes that

Owen would oppose his father instead of sitting there and taking it."
She told of how father complains, "You interfere with my punishing
of the children." Mother feels father interprets everything wrong.

After three visits with Owen's mother, the school system counselor had the following to say:

On the first visit, mother seemed intelligent, relaxed, and warm. Her
two young, pre-school daughters related to me readily. However, in
the last two interviews, the little girls' demands for attention from
mother and me were so great that they made the interview almost
impossible. Mother had so little control over the children that one
of them had quite a severe temper tantrum in retaliation to her
demands.
Mother shows a protective attitude toward Owen which becomes
greater as the crisis heightens. This attitude seems to exist not only
in relation to the school, but also at home where mother feels that
father is too stern with the boy. She tries to listen to the boy's story,
but father takes a distrustful attitude without question. Mother admitted that she and father disagree strongly about discipline methods
—as her own parents did. Her father was very strict and her mother
would soothe her with a glass of milk after she had been scolded
by him. Mother, too, had severe temper tantrums at Owen's age and
overcame them; she attributes the tantrums to the fact that her sister
got so much more attention than she did.
The helpfulness of my relationship with Owen in my twenty-two
half-hour interviews with him was hampered by his inability to face
his problem. He was continually teasing and testing me. He would
enter the room in a playful fashion and then leave, continually testing time limits. When I tried to be more directive in focusing on the
problem, he withdrew into working on his clay.

From the psychiatrist's interview with Owen's father we have
this report:

Father is an exactly dressed and well-groomed man who is exceedingly guarded. He believes that Owen's trouble is that he bottles up
his anger too long and then explodes. He wishes Owen would fight
back directly. He believes that there is nothing the matter with
Owen except that his mother babies him. About his own life he says
that he is doing rather menial work now. Although he has a bache-
lor's degree in accounting, he is working as a clerk. "I have trouble
on jobs. They have it in for me."

From these reports we see that Owen lives in a home atmosphere heavily laden with projection of blame. The mother blames the father and the school and the father blames the mother. Neither parent has insight into his or her own contribution to the problem. Not surprisingly, the counselor finds that Owen is not able to face his own problems. We can see the mechanics of the proejction of blame more clearly in the mother since we have more information about her. She obviously is continuing with her own children the modes of child rearing her own mother carried on. Just as she was sheltered from the stern limits of reality by her soothing mother, she shelters her children from the realities of the demands imposed by father. In this particular case, father's demands are exaggerated due to his own emotional disturbances. However, mother, due to her own exaggerated emphasis on freedom from controls and limits, cannot extract what is useful in father's disciplinary methods, but reacts against them blindly.

The picture is less diffuse in the case of Paul, a nine-and-a-half-year-old non-learner. His parents get along well together; neither one blames the other. Instead, the mother blames the school. The school report reads:

Paul's problem is that he is restless and inattentive; he annoys and bites others, often without cause. He says that the others picked on him first. His frequent sex play indicates that he has more than a normal interest in and preoccupation with sexual development. As for his academic work, he is a non-reader and does not do the required work. His I.Q. is 98. He is doing average work in handwriting, oral English, social studies, and science; he is barely passing in arithmetic, and is failing in reading, spelling, and written English.

The social worker gives the following report on Paul's mother:

Mother is a refined woman with prematurely gray hair. She speaks easily and well, but is unable to follow through with any discussion of her own involvement with the patient's problem. She came to the clinic at the suggestion of the principal, and when asked what the problem was and how the Institute might help, she replied indignantly that if she knew what the problem was, she would not be here.

Paul attended kindergarten at the age of five, but did not seem to adjust as early as the other children. He was eager to begin first grade, but mother noticed that he was not learning the alphabet. He was held over for a second year. He did well in the second grade, but in the middle of the third grade, the teacher began to complain that he was highly aggressive. Mother says she does not think that the teacher liked children, and that they certainly did not like her. Mother describes Paul's present teacher as "an old maid type," whom she says she dislikes. At the end of the interview, mother was able to become a little more reflective and said she guessed that Paul resents something which he is covering up and that she does not know whether or not it has anything to do with her or his father.

The psychiatrist wrote this of the mother:

Mrs. C. is a coldly attractive woman who says all the right things about child development and becomes extremely hostile and disconcerted whenever any of her feelings are discussed. For example, when she was asked if the boy's sex play made her feel uncomfortable, she became very defensive and said, "I don't see what this has to do with the child." She described a normal, happy home life with her husband, who is a research chemist and a good father.

The mother's defensiveness about her own and her husband's contribution to the problem prevents us from learning why she behaves as she does. In contrast to the previous case, where the mother's psychodynamics were easily observed, in this case we see only a cloak of proper normality, total denial of self-blame, and fault-finding with the school's educational methods. Her sharp, angry reaction to having her motives questioned makes us speculate about what the boy would be up against if he complained to mother about some of her own actions toward him. His anger to her must be bottled up and carried to school for ventilation. Moreover, he has learned from her that an aggressive self-whitewashing is a good means of coping with the world.

Learners.—Turning now to the learner group, we encounter Ronald, a nine-year-old. Having an I.Q. of 108, he does very well in reading, average in arithmetic, spelling, and English. However, as the school report states, "Ronald was so disturbed about his home situation that he went through periods of uncontrolled behavior. This was so extreme that he disrupted the entire classroom with his temper outbursts. He had to be sent to the Juvenile Detention Home."

The home situation is indeed disturbed. Mother and father separated two years ago and Ronald was placed in a boarding school by mother. In the interview with the psychiatrist, Ronald complained bitterly of his unhappiness in being away from home and not being visited by his mother. At times, his criticism of mother for neglecting him overwhelms him, and he begins to defend her, searching for statements he can make to her credit such as, "My mom brings me lots of nice things." In the interview he stood up the doll family of father, mother, brother, and sister, made them raise their hands as he threatened them with a pistol, and then methodically shot them, knocking them down with the point of his pistol; then he was ready to leave.

Mother, according to the social worker, is a woman who alternates ingratiation with irritation. She also vacillates between refusing to see that Ronald has a problem and blaming it on her ex-husband and on the adversities of life. She is well aware that Ronald wants to be at home with her, and spends most of her time excusing herself for not having him there. She says she has financial difficulties and medical troubles at present, and that she had to put up with her no-good husband in the past. "There is not really too much wrong with Ronald; the only trouble at home is that sometimes he is over-talkative and I have to shut him up." She is quite suspicious about what went on at the boarding school he attended, and she says that the grown-ups there probably did not supervise the boy enough. She does not plan to marry again because she despises men. Although she says her former mate was a wonderful husband for five years and did all the shopping and housework for her, he gradually changed and began to drink. In spite of her pleas that he return to being the kind of husband he was, he left her. She planned to find another boarding school for her son, since her working prevents her from taking proper care of him.

In Ronald's case we see a mother who disavows her lack of

concern for her children and her inabilities as a homemaker. Instead, she projects these faults on her husband who, according to her, deserted the family and deserted his responsibilties of doing the shopping and housework for her. The resulting build-up of hostility in Ronald is quite evident. Since his mother refuses to accept his criticisms of her neglect of him, he cannot maintain hate of her for long. Although he knocks down the doll family with pistol fire, his residual hostility and guilt about these feelings forces him into explosive, disruptive behavior at school, which damages himself as well as others.

These three cases illustrate the interrelationships between the mother's disinclination to see her role in the boy's problem, and the boy's tendency toward hostile, aggressive behavior. Whether the mother picks the father or the school as her scapegoat—or in other cases her in-laws, the neighbors, or her own parents—the repercussion on the boy is generally the same. He not only develops hostility because he is frustrated in making his needs clear to her, but he has learned to deny his own contribution to life events and to regard the other person as the aggressor.

One might think that only good would result if the mother dropped her blaming, scapegoating tendencies and faced up to her contribution to the problem. For the most part, this is true. Mothers of both groups who were not given to strongly blaming the father, the school, etc., more often had sons who were described by the school as mixing well with other children or as being co-operative with the teacher. However, as we approach the other end of the spectrum, the self-accusing mothers, we discover a different result in the sons. Frequently these boys are described by the school as shy, submissive, and anxious to please. Although this reaction is much less frustrating and exasperating to the teacher, it may represent a problem to the boy. The submissive-appearing boy has apparently learned that the best way of getting along with the aggressor is to blame oneself. The relationship between a self-accusing mother and her son can be seen in Hugh, an eight-year-old learner who was referred to the Institute because of bedwetting. Hugh has an I.Q. of 112 and is doing average work in reading, spelling, and penmanship. He is described as a "very quiet child, who is overly serious, mixes well with the group, and is submissive and shy with the teacher. He is happy when successful with his studies, and quite dejected when he doesn't reach his usual standards."

The social worker's notes about mother reveal the following:

Hugh's mother is well dressed. She appears quite anxious and depressed. When asked how the Institute could help, she said, "I feel that I must have some part in this. You may be able to tell me how to handle my children." Concerning the boy's bedwetting, she says she has tried persuading, scolding, and threatening, but believes that it might be better for her to put her arms around him and give him affection. When she goes into his room at night and sees him lying on his wet bed, she often sits on the side and cries, wondering where she has failed.

The case of Donald, a ten-year-old non-learner, is similar. He has considerable difficulty with all subjects and has repeated one grade. His teacher reports that he gets along well with other children but is meek and submissive with her.

In the psychiatric interview, he was quite deliberate, careful in speech and in his handling of the toys. He feels that both of his parents love him very much and, although he receives punishment from both of them, he feels it has been when he needed it. It bothers him that he and his brother can't stop fighting because that makes his parents irritated at them, and the boys with each other. From the social worker's interview we have this report of the mother:

She presents an unhappy and troubled expression. She says she is in constant distress from knowing that her own conflicts influence the children and feeling unable to do anything to help herself or them. She knows what is right but cannot do it. At times she almost wishes she did not know and could take things as they come. She once consulted a psychologist for ten visits. It was about a marital problem. Father had a terrible temper which was discouraging to mother. Moreover, he is a highly critical person. The psychologist taught mother to feel that in marriage the woman has 90 per cent of the adjustment to make, and that, since her husband was like this, she must put up with him and build her and the children's lives around the fact that he has a critical nature and bad temper. When the Institute's social worker asked her if she did not question the therapist's solution, she said, "Oh, no; she was not the kind of person one ever expressed an opinion to. You just did what she said and asked no question."

As these two cases illustrate, a guilty, self-accusing mother is more likely to have a submissive son. Taken together with the first three cases, these cases indicate that one factor influencing the presence of hostile, aggressive behavior in the son is the way in which the mother handles her own faults. At one end of this spectrum is the mother who overcomes her feelings of inadequacy and guilt by projecting the "bad" things onto others and being aggressively critical of that projected "bad." Her son utilizes this technique—technically called "identification with the aggressor"—and, fault-free, initiates hostilities which he claims are the fault of others. At the other end of the spectrum is the mother who pre-empts for herself more blame than is realistic. She and her son are more influenced in their behavior by feeling, "What have I done wrong?" than by asking "What have they done wrong?"

Aggression and Learning

In considering the relation of aggression to actual learning, we must begin with a central finding: Most of the non-learner boys were described either as aggressive or submissive in the classroom. On the other hand, most of the learner boys were described as co-operative with the teacher and as getting along well with the classmates. (See Table XVIII, page 192.) It would seem from this finding that learning difficulties are not simply associated with too much open aggression, but rather with the extremes of aggressiveness and submissiveness. Furthermore, it would seem that co-operativeness—a proper blending of aggressiveness and submissiveness—is a distinct aid in the learning process.

This finding and its explanation are in keeping with learning theory. In order to learn, one must have enough free aggressive energy to be inquisitive, to penetrate, and to persevere against obstacles. One must feel enough angry frustration in order to cope stenuously with an unsatisfying situation. But too much anger is not conducive to problem-solving; we see this in the child who destroys a puzzle he cannot put together. Moreover, too little angry displeasure is not conducive to learning; an example is the child who gives up apathetically or escapes when faced with frustration. Both aggressiveness and submissiveness— —when expressed to extremes—are harmful to the learning processes. But which is worse? If we use high intelligence scores and reading ability as indicators of good learning capacity, we would have to say that too *little* anger appears to have a worse effect on learning than does too *much* anger.

The overly aggressive non-learner, it appears, is intellectually brighter than the overly submissive non-learner. (See Tables XIV and XX, pages 190, 193.) The intelligence of the very aggressive boy possesses one component of a critic: namely, a strong capacity to sense what is unsatisfying if not actually wrong about the external world. This world does not gratify his needs and fantasies; therefore it is "bad" and should be attacked. The aggressive boy is not, however, intellectually brighter than the co-operative boy. If we turn to the learner group, we find that not only did the overly aggressive learners score no higher than the co-operative learners on the intelligence tests, but that they were more frequently described as "not working up to capacity." (See Table XXI.) It would seem, then, that while too much aggression is more conducive to learning than is too much submission, it does interfere with the boy's utilizing his full intellectual potential.

Reading Problems

The ability to read is the most basic intellectual tool for gaining knowledge about the world. It can be interfered with by neurological disease, visual defects, by emotional disturbance, etc. The measurement of reading disability is not always easy and depends on some kind of reading achievement test.

In this study, we have diagnosed reading disability simply on the basis of gross clinical signs. We did not use reading achievement results, since achievement tests were not given in all cases, and resorted instead to the schools' descriptions of how much difficulty the boys had had with reading and how much special help in reading they had required. Thus, when we speak of reading problems, we shall be referring to those boys who had at least two of the following three statements made about them by their schools: (1) he is failing in reading; (2) he has received special help in reading; (3) he should receive special help in reading. Using these criteria, about 50 per cent of the boys had reading problems.

Among these boys, we found that the greatest number were non-aggressive and passive (75 per cent). This finding accords with the experiences with other investigators. What was unexpected, however, was that as the aggressivity of the boys increased, reading problems did not decrease. While the middle, mixed group showed a low incidence of reading difficulties (26 per cent), the overly aggressive boys showed a sharp increase in the occurrence of reading problems (56 per cent).

An implication of these findings is that *reading problems are associated with both extremes of aggressive tendencies—too little and too much—rather than with a simple lack of aggressivity.* We have observed something of how these extremes originate and how they generally affect the boys. The main familial

factor is concerned with how the mother handles her own critical, blaming, fault-finding tendencies. Does she turn them against
the external world or against herself? We find, as we move
from the mothers of the non-aggressive boys, through mothers
of the mixed group, to mothers of the overly aggressive group
that there is a straight-line increase of mothers finding fault with
others and a straight-line decrease of mothers finding fault
with themselves.

Here we get some clue as to the origin of the sharp brightness
of the aggressive boy. His critical "mote in the other person's
eye" type of intelligence derives at least in part from his parents'
tendency to find fault with others. He has identified with a
mother who preserves her self-esteem by being critical of others
—by attacking her spouse if she is incompatible with him. Like
his mother, he has a hyper-awareness of the inevitable weak-
nesses and errors of the external world which he utilizes to put
the environment on the defensive and compel it to give him what
he wants. In moderate doses, such an awareness is intellectually
useful for being realistic and for detecting errors to be cor-
rected. In excessive dosage, however, it frequently results in
cynicism and sterile iconoclasm.

From the main factor of the mother's handling of her own
aggressive critical tendencies stem a number of important considerations. They will help us to understand the emotional climate
in which the aggressive and non-aggressive boys live and the
inner anxieties they have. Let us take first the critical mother
who blames others. We have said she does this to preserve her
self-esteem. We mean that in order to continue to admire, like,
or love herself, she has to project her "bad" attitudes onto others.
The central feature about her is that she needs a constant supply
of love and admiration from herself or from others. She is more
afraid of an interruption in that supply than she is of her anger
and violence. Her loves and hates tend not only to be strong,
but can alternate quickly. Her loving over-estimation of a person
can change to angry depreciation if that person fails to feed her

self-esteem. The boy, then, is exposed to a highly charged and flutuating maternal atmosphere in which he may be a fair-haired hero one day and a goat the next day. He, in turn, becomes fearful that his own love supplies may be diminished or cut off at any moment. He also will be angry if this frustrating event occurs.

We see a different picture in observing the mother who tends to find fault with herself. Although she might possibly be doing this to enhance her self-esteem indirectly, the more direct explanation is that she is more afraid that her violent anger might erupt than she is of having her love supplies cut off. She feels that even mild, realistic criticism of another would open a Pandora's box of violence within her that would lead to the destruction of the other person. Furthermore, in order not to have these feared impulses stimulated into activity, she cannot easily allow others around her to act in a destructive, messy, or violent way. The impact of all this on the son is especially pronounced since he, in his development, tends to be typically more aggressively violent than is a daughter. An early damper is placed on his insurgent masculinity; he must be polite, neat, and well-controlled much before he is ready to be that way. Like his mother, he becomes afraid of his own violent impulses and tries instead to be pleasant and obliging. This special impact on the son may explain, in part, why learning problems are much more frequent in boys than in girls.

This theoretical discussion serves as an introduction to the clinical material. We shall limit ourselves to descriptions of the boys with reading problems. Thus, we shall be describing first the aggressive non-reader and second, the non-aggressive or passive non-reader.

The Overly Aggressive Non-Reader

The prominent characteristics of these boys are hostile aggressiveness, fearfulness, increased eating, and an inability to tolerate change, separation, or dislocation. The last mentioned characteristic is probably the basic one from which the others issue. The blaming, fickle mother, who needs to protect her own supplies of self-love, produces considerable uncertainty in the boy about her reliability. Any change or dislocation in his environment reactivates his fear of separation from the mother. Upon separation, the boy is alone and fearful. As a substitute for the unreliable mother, he resorts to food. To combat the fearful, threatening apparition—the kind a small child sees when he is alone in the dark—he becomes aggressive. Aggressiveness is a sanctioned outlet in a turbulent, blaming family; it does not make the parent uneasy.

The case of Bernard, eleven, may serve as an illustration. The school report reads:

Bernard is exceedingly restless and disturbing in school, and is not making satisfactory progress. He is in the fifth grade because of age and not because of scholastic achievement. He is practically a non-reader, though he supposedly has a mental age of thirteen years and eight months. This is the third school he has attended. He does not live within our school boundaries, but was transferred here on permit because his conduct at the other school became unbearable to his teachers there.

The report further reveals that in spite of an I.Q. of 126, he is failing in reading, arithmetic, and spelling, and has had tutoring in reading. When he fails at some learning task, he either flies into a rage or becomes sullen and refuses to try again. He interferes with other children, makes excessive demands for the teacher's attention, and is defiant and impudent to her.

The early dislocation to which Bernard was exposed seems extreme. When he was an infant, his parents were separated and then divorced. Later they remarried but again were divorced. The three children were boarded out while mother went to work. Later mother and the children lived with mother's mother. When Bernard was seven, he suffered another separation. His older brother was run over by a truck and killed. As mother tells it, "Tom had been my favorite. He was the one who was most affectionate, would tell me how pretty I looked and would do things to help me. Tom was motherly to Bernard and for this reason Bernard took his death very hard." Bernard would get out of his bed at night, come into the living room and carry on a conversation between himself and his dead brother. He began to sleep better after mother bought him a panda which he would take to bed with him. Even though Bernard had difficulty getting along with other children before his brother's death, his school work had been good. He was six-and-a-half when he began first grade, and it was in this grade that he began to read. It was the following summer that his brother was killed, and from that time on, Bernard had marked difficulty in reading.

Mother's need to be given to and admired is evident from the above description. Moreover, according to her, her marriage failed because of her husband's brutality. She works now in a cleaning shop and keeps herself very busy. She complains that Bernard comes into the shop and interrupts her. She tries to give him the "brush-off" but he only "clings" all the closer. Mother says he seems to have a great need for cakes, candy, "just stuffing himself with sweets."

Regarding his fearfulness, the following incident is pertinent. Before mother and father finally separated, they had violent quarrels. Once after such a quarrel, mother could not find Bernard. After a long search, she found him in a room that was being redecorated. He was sitting in the corner in the dark, holding his panda and looking very frightened. Fearfulness was also noted in the psychiatric interview. The boy was startled easily by a bell ringing, and said he was always afraid of doctors. Although he said he would like to become an electrical engineer, he does not want to invent because he does not want to get killed. He would like to have a trained electric eel because it would kill enemies with an electric shock if they bothered him.

The case of Bernard is especially illustrative since it contains all the main characteristics previously mentioned, and also indicates the relation of separation or dislocation to reading difficulty.

In the other aggressive non-readers, some of these same characteristics may be seen. Peter, eleven years old, for example, evidences reaction to change and fearfulness. He had had no difficulties in the first grade, but in the second grade, an upsetting dislocation occurred when he had three different teachers. His reading difficulties became obvious then, and the teachers recommended to mother that he attend a reading clinic. Peter's association of separation and fearfulness is shown in a dream he had in the hospital while recovering from a ruptured appendix. He dreamed that a small "tough guy" was climbing on his bed, and that was the same night his mother and father had not come to visit him. His fearfulness was also evident in his reluctance to attend gym class because the scar from his appendectomy might open up. He is also frightened when he watches "scary" pictures on television. He was once afraid to go to a garage alone and had to have another boy go with him. He tells his mother, "I'm afraid so much."

Kenneth is a very aggressive nine-year-old. He steals money from other children and his teacher, and is disliked by the other children because he teases. He is failing in reading although he has an I.Q. of 122. Dislocation is evident in Kenneth's background. His mother reported that he was moved around a good deal during his earlier years and had to learn two languages, English and Norwegian. Finally, he spoke nothing but Norwegian until he was almost of school age, but at this time the family returned to America and he had to learn English. He had some difficulty in adjusting in the first grade, but in the second grade, he did better and liked his teacher very much. However, the family moved again, and he had to change schools. At this time, Kenneth began to get into difficulties again and would light matches in the basement and under his bed. He has become quite sensitive; when he is criticized, he becomes very upset and moody, and he holds grudges.

The case of Phillip, eight, shows the relation between separation and an increased emphasis on food. The school report says, "Phillip is restless, inattentive, and annoys others; he is a non-reader. He fights others—often without cause." He was adopted at the age of eight months; before that he had been in two foster homes. When he was three, his parents adopted a girl. The adoptive mother describes him as a voracious eater. In the psychiatric interview Phillip said, "I always drink my milk straight down, but my sister plays with the bottle. I'm the milk drinker in our family." He said he was "born from another mother and father and put into a place where babies are kept when people can't take care of them." When asked to make up a story about the doll family, he appeared frightened, and then he said he could think of a funny story. His story, which emphasized separation and food, is the following:

Mother, father, and baby were riding in a jalopy. A jack-knife fell out of father's pocket and baby cut a hole in the seat. Mother fell through and the sandwiches fell through after her. Then baby pulled out the gas pedal, brake, and steering wheel. They ran out of gas and there wasn't any food. The baby went home, but there wasn't any food, so he went to the next house and sneaked food out of the refrigerator.

The story ended when a snake bit mother and father drowned himself because the baby had left them.

The last example of aggressive non-readers is Richard. In this case, the teacher is aware that the boy is keenly intolerant of change of any kind. If he is moved from one seat to another, he becomes quite distressed, reacting more strongly than one would expect. This reaction to dislocation seems to have originated in a conflict between Richard's mother and grandmother over the boy's eating. At the age of three, when he was beginning to feed himself, mother would give him his food and he would eat it; then grandmother would come in and insist on feeding him with a spoon, saying that the baby was not getting enough to eat. Mother would object, and grandmother would respond angrily, "Well, if that's the way you feel about it, I'll have nothing to do with it." In the course of all this confusion, Richard would start crying. Grandmother finally left the house when the boy was six.

The Passive Non-Reader

The characteristics of passive non-readers are quite different and less dramatic. Not only are these children passive, friendly, and compliant—rather than antagonistic—but they also rarely have marked reactions to separation, fearfulness, or increased eating. For them, the family atmosphere is controlled and conformity is expected; the boy's only discernible resistance shows up in the form of constipation. (See Table XXIII, page 193.) Open aggression is not sanctioned; violence, messiness, and un-co-operativeness make the mother uneasy. Whereas the aggressive boy reacts to separation and neglect with angry protest, the passive boy strives to obtain the mother's love by accommodating himself to her wishes.

The case of Franklin illustrates some of these features. He is a ten-year-old boy with an I.Q. of 105. He has repeated two grades, and according to the teacher, "is unable to read even at a first-grade level." He is submissive to the teacher and accepted by the group. The psychiatrist describes him as a small boy, neatly dressed in a long-trouser suit. "Throughout the play interview he was very careful not to soil his suit, and he never did remove his coat."

Controlling, anti-aggressive attitudes emanate from both of Franklin's parents. The psychiatrist says about his mother:

At no time was Mrs. P. openly hostile or critical. She was consistently defensive, allowing no expression of her own feelings. When I tried to evoke some feeling about her excessive burden—which included a home, five children, and a full-time job—she simply said she was used to it.

About Franklin's father the psychiatrist writes:

Mr. P. is a serious, soft-spoken individual, who exerted every effort to control himself rigidly so that the impression he made would be absolutely correct. He admitted that he was too strict with the children and gave them too many beatings when they were very young. He described how this error was brought home to him when he noticed one day how the children stopped playing when he walked into the room.

Franklin's accommodating behavior manifested itself quite early in life. As his mother tells it:

He was an awfully good baby; he had to be because I had three older children below the age of three. His next older brother was very sick with diarrhea, so Franklin did not get as much care as he should have. He was such a good baby, and so quiet, that one summer when I was visiting my brother, we left him on the sewing machine in his bassinet and almost drove off without him.

He would play by himself for hours in the play-pen without demanding attention. At present, he frequently daydreams and talks to imaginary playmates. His mother started his toilet training quite early because she wanted to train him with an older sibling. Although it was successfully completed, Franklin now has a tendency to be constipated.

Similar features may be seen in the case of Wilson, a seven-year-old passive non-reader. The school report says:

Wilson lacks ability to grasp school work; he is no problem otherwise, being very co-operative in everything except school work. He may lack ability—or at least lack the ability to use his intelligence. He has not responded well to remedial reading but has more confidence in reading while maintaining physical contact with the teacher, and wants to have her arm around him.

In the psychiatric interview, he was co-operative but lacked spontaneity. Rather than play with the toys and get dirty, he drew a car on a piece of paper and was very meticulous in drawing all the little details.

In Wilson's family, the mother—not the father—keeps the lid on aggressive feelings. Mother says father is easygoing and will not discipline the children. He often sends them to mother for permission to do things instead of having them take more responsibility for what they do. Mother's emphasis on responsibility prevents her from being more openly resentful of the situation in which she finds herself. She has eleven children and is expecting a twelfth. She acknowledges that she has been feeling "more upset and anxious" than usual, "getting very nervous so that I can't bear the over-crowded living quarters." She has headaches and her nails are badly bitten. She guesses that the real trouble is simply that she is pregnant again. Thus, instead of utilizing open anger, mother, fearing her own violence, has to use substitute aggressive outlets like nail-biting and headaches.

Another variety of anti-aggressive behavior may be seen in seven-year-old Theodore, a passive non-reader who is also having considerable trouble with arithmetic. The teacher reports:

Teddy is an only child. I think his trouble stems chiefly from the fact that he has very little opportunity to play with other children of his own age. His mother brings him in the morning, calls for him at lunch, brings him back, and then calls for him at the end of the day. After school hours he apparently spends his time in the house with his mother where he is continually reminded to be quiet so as not to disturb the other people who occupy the same house.

Mother's fear of giving offense also evidenced itself in the interview with the social worker, who writes:

Mother is apologetic in her manner, not sure that she should be here taking our time when there are so many other parents who need our help. Her solicitous overprotection of Ted stems from her self-blaming tendencies. Two weeks before he was born, the doctor discovered that she had diabetes. She was so ill that the doctor feared for both her and the baby. For two years following, she was weak and tired, and could not devote full attention to the baby. She feels quite guilty about this neglect.

Ted's avoidance of overt aggression was neatly illustrated in the psychiatric interview. The psychiatrist reports that Ted told him the following fantasy:

A pet dog of the family was shot and bleeding profusely. Ted went up to the dog and nudged him. In so doing, he got himself covered with blood. His mother became very angry because he was all mussed up. At this point in the story, Ted backed away from the very little bit of sawdust he had produced by his sawing activity saying that he would "really get it good"—motioning to his neck— if he got himself dirty in the playroom.

Our final example is that of Gordon, a nine-year-old passive non-reader. Here, the controlling of the mother, the anti-aggressive compliance of the boy, and the effects of this on the bowel function of the boy are well illustrated. The school reports state:

Gordon is a very poor reader. He seems to have lapses of memory. He knows a simple word one minute and forgets it the next. He is not a discipline problem. His younger sister is a very good reader and student.

Mother is quite disturbed about his reading problem. Despite special tutoring and the fact that he was placed back a grade with a wonderful teacher, his reading has not improved. When Gordon first began to have reading difficulty, his mother spent much time trying to teach him but had no success. The social worker notes that the mother is quite well groomed and tends to speak in a precise manner. She does most of the disciplining.

The mother's attitude toward her own hostile feelings is quite pertinent here. Though she is capable of lashing out upon great provocation, she feels guilty and condemns herself afterward. This tendency is seen in the mother's statements made in her interview with the social worker:

"Gordon is such a good boy except in reading. I tried to help him so hard that maybe I did more harm than good." When she was trying to tutor him, mother became so upset that she would scream at him, and then in a temper strike him and call him "dummy." As mother told of her inordinate temper reaction, she began to cry. She immediately clamped down on this show of feeling, and -then said defensively, "Don't get me wrong, he's really not a disappointment to us. He's good; he's clean; he respects; and he is very lovable."

Mother's emphasis on the desirable quality of cleanliness is borne out by the other major symptoms Gordon has. For the last two years, he has been constantly "itchy in his rectum." This trouble seems to have originated in the boy's earliest years. He was not planned for and was born ten months after the marriage. Mother had intended to continue working at a job she liked for a number of years. At any event, according to mother, Gordon was toilet-trained "when very young." He was completely out of diapers during the day at fourteen months and completely trained at night at twenty months. Mother trained him by taking him to the bathroom at fifteen-minute intervals. She recalled that when Gordon occasionally had an accident he went to get a rag to wipe it up. He had chronic constipation, his bowel movements being frequently hard and dry. Gordon also displayed an exaggerated tendency to accommodate himself when he showed no reaction to the abrupt weaning he experienced when his sister was born (he was two) or to the family's moving to their own house when he was five. As the mother put it, "Gordon took all of this in his stride."

The foregoing examples illustrate the different emotional situations of overly aggressive and passive non-readers. The aggressive non-reader appears to come from a family climate of potential separation or dislocation. His aggressive energies are not inhibited, but appear to be diverted to non-learning channels—such as bidding for more attention, attacking real rivals and imagined enemies, and building up his own power. The passive non-reader appears to come from family climate unfavorable towards violence and messiness and pressing for conformity and cleanness. The boy's aggressive energies *are* inhibited; permission is given only for safe, conventional, "nice" outlets. Reading and the intellectual adventure of ideas may make one dangerously unconventional and non-conforming. In line with this, it will be recalled that the burning of books is a frequent political technique of a dictatorship insistent on absolute conformity. However, in the families in which there are no threats of dislocation and no severe sanctions against aggression, boys find the necessary security and freedom to engage comfortably in reading and learning.

Part Two

SUPPLEMENTARY

CLINICAL

STUDIES

FAILURE AT THE

COLLEGE LEVEL

*i*N PART TWO, we shall view learning problems occurring outside of our study group. The learners and non-learners
discussed in Part One were in the age range of seven to sixteen,
had a minimum I.Q. of 90, and were seen for diagnostic interviews. The case material presented in Part Two goes beyond
these limits. However, we shall introduce no new learning factors here. Instead, we intend merely to show that the factors
already described may be helpful in understanding other boys
with learning difficulties. For the most part, the cases are randomly drawn from the author's clinical experience. Because they
do not derive from a systematic study, they will be used to
illustrate rather than to prove.

In this short chapter, our concern will be with three older
youths who have failed in college. They are of special interest
because they may inform us about what can happen to the
bright *learners* in our study group.

We shall find that not all the factors we have discussed figure
prominently in explaining the failures of these three young men.
The adverse effect of lower-class origin is nil since all come from
the middle- or upper-middle-class. Double family disorganization
(marital discord *and* a working mother) is also missing as a de-

terminent. That these factors are absent is not surprising, for these youths have had a good start educationally. They come from a social class which values education, supplying them with motivation, and their homes were secure enough that they could master the basic tool subjects and go on to deal with more abstract matters.

The factors that do play a part are less gross. They are those which can frequently be found in the average American middle-class or upper-middle-class home—some degree of marital discord, unwise ambitiousness of the parents, and high or low expectations of maturity. They operate singly or in combination to render the young man relatively incapable of utilizing his proven capacity for learning. This occurs at a time when he appears to be just one step from making his way in the world. For persons with more severe learning problems, the time of crisis is much earlier. Going from home to kindergarten is too big a step for some; leaving grade school for high school is an overly difficult one for others. With these young men, the earlier steps had been successfully managed—intellectually if not emotionally. Their crisis occurred at college entrance and at graduation.

If there is any common feature in these three cases, it is the anxiety which overwhelms the learning apparatus when the young man realizes he has to compete aggressively with others. Competition reactivates early primitive fears such as, "If you wish to kill, then others may wish to kill you—and furthermore, because of your wish, you deserve to be killed." Up to now, these young men have avoided facing the reality of competition by such competition-avoiding devices as a grandiose conviction that no one else really measures up to them, an overly low self-estimate, or a feeling that one has much time in college before deciding on a definite career. If these devices work, anxiety may be held down—despite the fact that it is easily apparent that they are not making much headway in their studies. When these devices fail, frequently such students feel a great upsurge of anxiety, sometimes approaching panic, which makes concentration impossible. Whether the anxiety is great or small, the central issue is most often that the young men fear to be successful in competition. For good reasons, then, this has been called a "success neurosis."

Ken, seventeen years old, had made an impressive record in high school. Graduating tenth in a class of over 300, he had been highly involved in extra-curricular activities, principally athletics. The football coach under whom he played was a hard-driving man who demanded perfection of the players. Ken was deputized as a sort of assistant coach and was made responsible for instructing the freshman players. He seemingly thrived on this added responsibility; only at times was he dimly aware of his fatigue and his resentment of the pressured schedule.

His acceptance of the deputy coach role could be explained by his family situation. He was the oldest of four brothers and was used to accepting responsibility. His only obvious emotional disturbance was shown in that, at the age of seven, he was seen by a child psychiatrist because of nightmares. His mother was very ambitious for him, his brothers, her husband, and herself. Her ideal was a man with dynamic drive. Unfortunately, her husband was a slower moving man who had undergone several business reverses and was consequently depressed. Ken's role in the family was to satisfy his mother's ambitions *and* to cheer up his depressed, pessimistic father. As we have said in an earlier chapter, the double role can be intensely conflictful. If Ken does satisfy his mother by being successful, then father's defeat in life will be poignantly accentuated. To spare his father this humiliation and also to ward off father's jealousy, Ken would have to fail.

The beginnings of Ken's failure during his first month at college were not apparent to anyone. But gradually his anxiety became more obvious. He could not concentrate on his studies; in tests he would begin to put down the correct answer, doubt it, and finally give a wrong answer. Restlessness and arguments with his roommate followed. He began calling home and would break into tears when talking with his parents. After an interview with a college counselor, he felt temporarily better, but soon took a turn for the worse.

At Christmas vacation, he was first seen by the present author. He was exceedingly restless, complained of stomach pains and nausea, told of hallucinations in which he heard the football coach commanding him to do things this way or that. Tearfully, he said he was "losing his father." The recommendation that he stop school was resisted by his parents. He returned to college, but within a week he was back home, and at this point, the parents recognized the boy's plight and the idea of therapy became more acceptable. As treatment proceeded and as his conflict was pointed out to him, Ken gradually relaxed and lost most of his symptoms. In a characteristic expression of his intense achievement needs, he enrolled in a part-time scholastic program at a local college within a month after beginning treatment.

Ken illustrates several of the factors discussed in earlier chapters. In particular, he exemplifies the conflict faced when the mother is ambitious for the son and the father is comparatively unsuccessful. Success for the son means "killing the father," hence Ken says that he has lost his father. He sees his identification with the driving football coach is another disloyalty to father. Resistance to ambition is not shown too clearly here, for Ken can scarcely afford not to achieve outwardly. His achievements in the last two years of high school, however, must be considered a tour de force during which Ken was operating much beyond his emotional reserves. Also seen here is the characteristic first-son psychology. Ken was leaned on by both parents and became a substitute parent on the football team. His nausea is of a kind frequently found in first-born children who resist pressured feeding by the mother.

Will, another seventeen-year-old, did not have a spectacular high school record. Although of superior intelligence, he graduated only in the upper third of his class. In some of his courses, his performance was indifferent; his teachers frequently told him that he could do much better. In spite of this record, and in spite of his own low self-estimate (he felt he wasn't too smart), he applied for and was admitted to an eastern college where the standards and competition were high and keen.

Why he did this is again explainable by the situation in his family. Will was the third and last child—the oldest was a brother, the next a sister. Both parents were ambitious, and the father was successful in this case. The theme of the family was productivity, which was preached principally by the father, a self-made man who, according to Will always had his "nose to the grindstone." Marital discord was intense; divorce had been contemplated several times, but never carried out. The mother had married principally for protection and security, and had had these desires well satisfied. However, she felt that her sensitive individuality was being trampled on by her insensitive, materialistic husband.

The father and the older brother formed one team; while Will and his sister were quite sympathetic to their mother's unhappiness. However, Will also wanted to be considered by his father and brother to be as intellectually adequate as they. His opinions and challenging remarks were beaten down by them, his father using a violent temper and disparaging remarks, his brother using his fists. With no intellectual support from anyone else in the family (his mother was afraid of his father), he began to develop the idea that he was as stupid as his father and brother claimed. Yet, in a wild hope that he could take his place with the senior men, he enrolled at the eastern college.

The onset of panicky anxiety came sooner for Will than it did for Ken. Within two weeks after beginning college, he became fearful, depressed, and thought continually of suicide. Pride in being self-reliant was not a strong factor: he reached out indiscriminately for help—from classmates, teachers, and his parents. Somehow he managed to hang on until Thanksgiving vacation, when, on returning home, he was seen for the first time by the author. No resistance was offered by him or his parents to the recommendation that he leave school. While treatment progressed, Will lived at home, not working or attending school. Even this protected situation was not safe enough for him, and he frequently asked to be sent to a mental hospital. Gradually he began to feel more adequate, and after a year and a half, he enrolled at a local college where the standards were not too demanding. Initially, he had many misgivings and was sure he was flunking the tests. He was surprised and even anxious when his papers came back marked "A." It developed that he was afraid of the reaction of his classmates to his high grades. He defended against their envy by telling them he was lucky or by not revealing what his grades were. In the past, he had defended against their envy by not daring to be right.

In Will's case, we see the factors of marital discord, low expectations of maturity, and ambitious family standards. Sympathetic to his aggrieved mother, he resented his father and older brother too much to use them as models for identification. Furthermore, his sympathizing mother had not expected much of her last-born except that he be close to her as a little boy. Yet, Will wished to be adequate as a man. If he knuckled under to his father and brother, he despised himself for being a coward. If he opposed them and confronted them with his successful achievement, he felt in danger of being attacked, depreciated, or, in primitive terms, castrated by them.

Our last young man is Peter, a twenty-year-old whose difficulties were delayed until his senior year of college. His high school academic record was especially distinguished and culminated in his winning a national scholarship. The momentum of these triumphs carried him through the first two years of college, but then he became uneasy. As he described it later, he felt like the character in the cartoons who runs off a cliff and runs through the air until he looks down and realizes there is nothing beneath him.

The most immediate event precipitating this lack of confidence was a rebuffing by a girl. This was not the usual disap-

pointment in love, but rather an ego blow. For on his second
date with her, she bluntly commented that he was acting like
a high school sophomore. This comment plunged him into a
deep depression. Up to this time, Peter had prided himself on
being very sophisticated, on being able to be taken for twenty-
five years old. Nothing in his life so far had occurred to dispel
this conviction. From childhood on, he had been accepted and
listened to by older people such as his parents' friends. And at
the experimental high school he attended, the age gap between
teacher and student had been "democratically" narrowed. This
background of adult acceptance plus his academic honors fed
the illusion that he had really arrived as a mature man. The illusion was rudely jolted, however, by the girl who told him, in
effect, that the king was naked.

Before the incident, Peter's doubts about his adequacy had
been growing. He dimly realized that he was not a self-starter.
When a goal or project was suggested to him by a teacher as
happened in high school and early college, he could work brilliantly and at times even arduously. But, when thrown on his
own, as he was later in college, he had no strong conviction
that he knew what was best for him. To defend against the
growing sense of inadequacy, he had erected a façade of overmaturity. Lending conviction to the façade were his interests
in travel and foreign languages. The surface picture he presented
—of a brilliant, cultivated, and cosmopolitan young man—was
accepted by many. But he did not wholly believe it, and of
course, the girl actually disbelieved it.

What lay behind Peter's lack of self-determination? From what
could be learned during his therapy with the author, the attitudes of his parents were chiefly responsible. Peter was the third
and last child of highly cultured parents. They were, however,
not especially ambitious for their children. Rather, their gratification derived from being over-valued by their sons. The father
did not encourage originality in his off-spring; he was more
gratified by being looked upon as the fount of wisdom. Though

ambitious for himself, he preferred that his sons be his disciples. The mother was not intellectually competitive with her children. Her way of being over-valued was to be emotionally necessary to them. She would spend much time and energy with whomever was weak, sick, and damaged—be that person one of her sons or a friend in need.

Peter, then, came from a family in which the rewards for being autonomous and self-determined were negligible. On the other hand, the emotional penalties could be considerable. Contesting father's opinions or his role as the originator of wisdom, would cost Peter his father's affection and might bring on a depreciating attack. Disengaging himself from mother's enveloping warmth would make her feel less important and him more isolated. In order not to see his parents as they really were— because this would result in emotional penalties—he idealized them. His father *was* very wise, his mother *was* very helpful. If he were really to grow up, he would displace his parents from these esteemed roles. His compromise was to act as if he was grown up and to remain basically dependent.

The factor involved here is low expectation of maturity. Although Peter's older brothers also suffered from their father's need to be an oracle and their mother's need to be over-maternal, the impact on last-born Peter was greater. The cultural standards of his family and his own superior intelligence enabled him to acquit himself admirably up to his junior year in college. But when it came time for him to replace pseudo-maturity with real autonomous maturity, his emotional preparation for this step proved to be woefully inadequate. He did not leave college in the highly anxious state we noted in the other two youths. Rather, in his junior year, he became increasingly depressed. Although maintaining a B average, he was certain that in his senior year his grades would go still lower. Rather than face this prospective defeat, he dropped out of college and sought psychiatric treatment. His progress in treatment continued for some time to be erratic. Like Will, he did not quickly go back to school.

A year went by (and he toyed with the idea of becoming a literary expatriate) before he came to grips with his problem in maturation and re-entered college.

With these excerpts, we have attempted to show how *some* of the factors operative in our non-learners and learners play a role in *some* college failures. As was said, the operative factors are subtle rather than gross. Except possibly in the case of Will, no one could have predicted with any degree of certainty that those youths would have any difficulties in college. There are undoubtedly many successful college students whose family backgrounds would reveal some marital discord, some unwise ambitions, and some excessively high or low expectations of maturity. Yet, using hindsight, we can see how these subtle factors contributed to the young men's failure. The situation is much like that in a physical disease such as pneumonia. Not everyone who is exposed to the germs will develop pneumonia. Still, in everyone who contracts the disease, the pneumococcus organism will be found. The parallel with learning is that, given a low resistance, an unusual combination or dosage of anti-learning factors will result in college failure. As in any illness, careful diagnosis is necessary to ward off or shorten the unfavorable process.

PROBLEMS OF

PRESCHOOL CHILDREN

*I*N CONTRAST to the comparatively subtle factors operating in college failures are the flagrantly chaotic home conditions which contribute to preschoolers' problems in learning and aggression. The two cases presented in this chapter have in common the severely disorganized home resulting from marital discord and a working mother. The effects we noted previously on boys over seven will be found again—but more graphically—in these boys of five and three.

An interesting side-facet of the home situation is its effect on the intelligence test scores: the first boy showed a rise from 78 to 108; while the second boy's score dropped from 119 to 75. Although test scores are not magically infallible in their predictive ability, experience has shown that they are generally a rather reliable measure of the boy's current intellectual functioning. In our study group, the non-learners had at least an I.Q. of 90, even though they were failing in school. In these two young boys, however, the disorganizing impact on the intellectual powers was such that, at one time or another, they were functioning as borderline mental defectives.

Our first boy is Keith, an only child of five. He came to the attention of the clinic because of his running away from home.

His distraught mother said that for the past month Keith had run away about three times a week. He would wander into other neighborhoods and would be returned by adults and the police. Because he did not know his address, his mother put a dog tag on him to facilitate his return.

His present symptoms had the following development. Six months previously, Keith had entered kindergarten. His mother had taken him and brought him home for the first two weeks. He attended from noon to 3 P.M., and his mother was then working from 4 to 12 P.M. Soon he started daytime wetting, apparently outside school hours since the teacher did not mention the problem. Mother was surprised by this because Keith had been fully toilet-trained at eight months and had never wet the bed.

After two weeks of school, his mother changed to the day shift, and Keith's aunt escorted him to school. By the time the aunt got home the first day, he was already back home saying that the school doors were locked. A week later, on a day his mother was off from work, he came home in the middle of school, saying that he was tired. After he did the same thing a week later, mother removed him from school, thinking she would wait until he was older.

A month later, she enrolled him in an all-day nursery school. On the second day, he objected to this, crying that he did not want to go in the car. He now began soiling as well as wetting, and has continued to wet two or three times a day and soil once a day regularly. Because of his continued objections, he was removed from the nursery school after two weeks.

For the last two months, he has not been in any school. When crossed in his desires, he has violent temper tantrums. Mother had not been overly concerned about the tantrums or the wetting and soiling, but when he began to run away from home, she became quite worried.

In the psychological testing situation, Keith was extremely restless, anxious, and distractible. Because of his tangential associations, it was continually necessary to reach out and hold his attention in order to bring him back to the task at hand. Examples of this anxious distractibility shown in these responses: "Do you know why I run away from the house? I'm scared of the cops; they put you in jail." At this point Keith began to cry, but stopped after some reassurance. Later, he asked, "Is there a mommey sleeping around here?" When asked why, he said, "I don't want to wake her up and go to jail."

His anxiety manifested itself in his associations to the intelligence test questions. When asked what one does when one cuts a finger, his first response was, "You don't have a finger left." When asked in what way a knife and a piece of glass were the same, he said that they would hurt a man or a girl—"they go way up in the air and cut a man's head off." A regressive retreat from the threatening world was seen in an answer to the Sentence Completion Test. When asked to complete the sentence beginning, "What I want most to do," he replied, "crawl back in bed."

On the Verbal Scale of the Wechsler Intelligence Scale for Children he earned an I.Q. of 70. This estimate was believed reliable but not valid because of the boy's extreme distractibility. In other words, although the score indicated the boy's current intellectual functioning, it did not reflect what he could do when free of distracting anxiety.

In the psychiatric examination, much the same anxious behavior was seen. At length, Keith settled down to paint and painted a dog which he called a bad dog. Successively, he changed this painting into other things by adding concentric lines of dark paint. Thus, it became a "big bear to scare you" and then "a wolf." After this, he fearfully and then more boldly shot the examiner with the toy gun.

When the boy's social history was taken, the mother revealed the disorganized home conditions giving rise to such anxiety and aggression in the boy. She was very resentful toward her husband, a machine operator eleven years older than she. "He did not want this child and didn't want any other because he doesn't want to be tied down. I only stay with him because of the boy." She related that he is very difficult to get along with, becomes physically abusive to her just like her father was to her mother, and supports Keith's defiance of his mother. Mother dislikes the arguments, which are often over money, because they make her stomach get "all tied in knots" and she vomits. Mother separated from father twice for brief periods, once making arrangements for divorce, but each time father persuaded her to come back. In order to escape the tension, mother began working part-time when Keith was two-and-a-half, leaving the boy in the care of her mother upon whom she was quite dependent.

The home conditions appeared so chaotic and lacking in remedy that the clinic first considered that placement of Keith outside of the home was the only possible solution. However, because of mother's anxiety and genuine concern for the boy, the staff believed that she might benefit from therapeutic interviews. Mother accepted this opportunity and faithfully kept her appointments for six months. The emotional support and understanding she derived reduced her anxiety and enabled her to cope with her husband and son less resentfully. Keith re-entered school and remained without running away. The only symptom that persisted was the soiling. On a re-test, Keith earned an I.Q. of 108. Mother stopped treatment after six months, saying that she felt that she had things better under control.

Our second case, Paul, three, also an only child, is similar to Keith's, but has a less happy ending. The urgency and flavor of the precipitating situation can be appreciated from the social worker's notes of mother's initial telephone call:

The mother called and talked in a childlike voice. She says Paul is terribly restless, wakes up at night, and sleeps little. He scratches his father when father is loving him. He picked up a piece of glass and ran with it after another child. He talks about burning the house down. He pokes at the eyes of the dog and is sadistic. He bumps into chairs when he walks around the house. Mother said that she didn't raise this child because she worked and left him in the care of his grandmother and other relatives.

The relatives always complained about him, but she would not believe them. She always had excuses for the boy and never really noticed the severe behavior until she started to take care of him herself after she stopped working six months ago. Now she can make no more excuses for him. She is most frightened by the incident of the piece of glass.

When Paul's mother was seen for the social history, she, with much pressure of speech, began by giving the background events. At the time Paul was born, she and her husband lived with her parents. There was so much friction that she told her husband she would leave him with the child and divorce him if he would not move out. He did move out, and soon they bought their present home. It became necessary for mother to work to help with payments for the home and furnishings. Paul was left with his grandmother, but she complained that he was too active and made her nervous. Mother finally had to take him back, but she still felt that she had to find someone to take care of her boy. Her sister-in-law took care of him for two days, and then mother found a family with whom she placed him. After six weeks, the woman said Paul made her too nervous and another home had to be found. Mother commented that she was not really worried about the many moves and changes: "After all, he was still a baby." Finally, the maternal grandmother took care of him again when mother worked nights. When Paul was at home, the mother would try to catch a few more hours of sleep and would lock the child in a room. Now he gets hysterical if she even closes a door and will not allow it under any conditions.

Although mother has not been working for the past six months, Paul is no better. She threatens him, fights with him, and argues. He wakes up every morning at two and calls for mother. He wets the bed. Mother bought him a dog because he was lonely, but she had to give it away because he hurt it. His sexual interests are also aggressive. He talks about mother's bust and grabs at her breasts. He also grabs at father's penis when they are in the bathroom together. In his play with trains and little dolls, he says the dolls are mommey and daddy and that the train ran over them.

In the psychological testing and in the psychiatric interview, the same aggressiveness was evident. The psychologist stated:

Immediately on entering the room, he showed signs of hyperactivity and impulsivity. At first, I could get him to stop to complete one test item. But as time went on, he became more negativistic and destructive; for example, he threw the test equipment on the floor and tried to tear the test equipment off the cards. He did his best to sabotage all efforts to test him correctly and finally said, "I won't listen to you. I listen to the devil."

In spite of all this behavior, he earned an I.Q. of 119 on the Revised Stanford-Binet Form L, showing particular facility in the verbal area.

In the psychiatric interview, he was again hyperactive and distractible. After using the toilet, he became very interested in flushing it and did this repeatedly. Once, after so doing, he inappropriately ran out and sat on the floor. There was no method to his play; he examined objects aimlessly without making use of them. His attention span seemed very short. He frequently asked questions about the switches on the wall, though it was repeatedly explained to him that they did not work.

The staff was dubious about what could be done for Paul. They objected to placement outside of the home because he had already suffered many changes and was so aggressively provocative that no ordinary home or institutional placement would be able to tolerate him. Because the mother seemed to be under considerable tension and had benefitted from ventilating her complaints, it was decided to see Paul and his mother in therapeutic interviews.

Due to other information mother gave about herself, the prognosis was quite guarded. In comparison to Keith's mother, Paul's mother appeared much more rejecting of her boy, of her husband, and of her own parents. She married father only to get out of her own home and to secure financial support. Although father is a hard worker, she looks down on his being a garage mechanic. She can control him with her complaints and depreciation, but she does not respect him. At times, because of his comparative lack of drive, she has called him the "scum of the earth." Ocasionally, she has thought of divorce or of seeing other men because she derives little sexual satisfaction from her husband.

However, mother felt most intensely about her own mother. She cried whenever she mentioned an instance of being neglected by her; she said it "broke my heart" to hear her mother say she looked like her father and was "just like her no-good father." Mother's father deserted the family and spent some time in prison and in a mental hospital. Her mother obtained a divorce and made a second marriage when Paul's mother was thirteen. The latter was placed in a relative's home where she felt she had to do all the hard work. She truanted from school and was finally placed in a boarding school where she felt happier.

Even at present, Paul's mother is hurt by her mother's not caring for her. She can't understand why she resents looking after her only grandson. Recently, she asked her mother why she didn't love her and the answer was, "I just can't help it." This so upset mother that she cried all night.

Because, then, of Paul's mother's disorganization, her woeful lack of preparation for motherhood, and because of her insistent childlike needs to be mothered herself, treatment began with a dubious prognosis. Adding caution to the outlook was the following report from the nursery school in which mother had recently enrolled Paul:

Mother and child arrived early on the appointed day and the child was a sight to behold. Both of them literally came crashing in with Paul in the lead and mother desperately trying to hang on to him.

Mother tried to make introductions but Paul was chasing, falling, and shouting, "Where are the toys?" Once in the room, he settled down somewhat, but then continually asked for help and for his mother to play with him. He was overly concerned with anything that was bent or broken. The mother was told that Paul would be given a two weeks' trial.

When Paul actually entered the school three days later, he seemed calmer. However, from the first day, he tried to molest the goldfish, saying he didn't like them. When one actually died some time later, he was very upset and repeated, "I didn't do it." At first, Paul paid exclusive attention to the teachers and ignored the other children. Later he found another boy with the same first name and tried to kiss, fondle, and hug this child and would moan his name over and over. Most of the time he would lean against one of the teachers and talk incessantly. During the third week he attended school, he wet his pants three to six times a day. He seemed not to understand the use of the bathroom. However, this behavior seemed explainable by the fact that his teacher announced to the children that she was going to Boston for a few days. Upon hearing this, Paul began to cry and scream. He said over and over again that he would be a good boy. Then he told the teacher how much he hated her and how angry he was. "I'm so angry at you I'm going to wet my pants."

Paul gradually calmed down and seemed to accept and trust the teacher. However, this may not last because his mother gives every indication of being a very anxious person—one day frantic, very tired and depressed the next. She seems to feel that the teacher has the magic formula for handling Paul and that they just won't tell her what it is. She asked every day how he was getting along and always seemed disappointed when we did not tell her he was "cured."

Treatment proceeded with weekly interviews for mother and child and lasted about two years. Constant themes during mother's treatment were her regarding of Paul as an extension of herself (his success and failures were her's) and her dwelling on the maternal and emotional hardships of her earlier life. Marital discord decreased but was not eliminated. Paul also showed some improvement; he managed to adjust at camp and remained in school full-time with moderately satisfactory preformance. In treatment, he became able to talk about the things that bothered him, rather than simply to act them out. When he did act aggressively, it was related to some specific precipitating event and was no longer the diffuse, distracted, and at times incomprehensible acting out in all directions which he exhibited previously.

Paul's progress is shown in a re-test of his intelligence one year after treatment began. The psychologists reported:

Paul responds well to controls and shows none of the provocative, defiant behavior exhibited on the first test. He does seem somewhat unco-ordinated at times, and, during periods of intense concentration, he will drool. However, we find no test signs of organic brain disease, and the neurological examination was negative. As he was tiring from the test, one bit of peculiar behavior was evidenced. He would suddenly scream out some phrase in a very automatic way. I was not even certain that he knew he had said anything, and after one such a scream, he looked at me in a very startled way, as though surprised at what had issued from his lips. Most often the phrases yelled were "good boy" and "smart boy," both echoes of comments I had made concerning his performance. He again earned an I.Q. of 118 on the Revised Stanford-Binet Form L. This estimate is considered minimal because he performs in a manner suggestive of very superior potential capacity.

At the time of this test, treatment had ended because mother was still not satisfied with less than magical formulae. The staff believed that although some gains had been made, much more treatment would be needed to consolidate them. The caution was well-warranted because after a year, mother reapplied for help. Paul was constantly in trouble in school, failing in his subjects, and the other boys called him a murderer because they suspected him of killing a rabbit. The teachers mistrusted him and he was becoming accident-prone; several times he cut himself so badly that stitches were taken. Mother and Paul were seen again for a few diagnostic interviews after which mother asked definitely for placement of Paul outside of the home.

Our final record of Paul comes from the intelligence test given him on his last visit to the clinic. In the examining situation, Paul was overly animated, impulsive, and extremely provocative. The examination was permeated with outbursts in which he would pound on the table, bring up extraneous bits of conversation, run across the room, snatch test materials, and make faces in the one-way mirror. Present intelligence tests results are markedly lower than the superior or high average ratings he earned previously. Now he earns an I.Q. of 80 on the Stanford-Binet and a 74 on the Arthur Performance Scale. It is difficult to determine how much this discrepancy is due to an actual decrease in ability to function at the present time or to a conscious effort to do poorly so he will be deemed in need of help at the clinic. Whatever the reason, the low score accounts for his current poor functioning in school.

The two cases illustrate the effects of severe family disorganization upon intellectual functioning and behavior. These effects are, of course, more vivid in preschoolers whose maturation has not been sufficient to provide them with suitable controls. The reader will recall that in our non-learner groups, the younger boys were much more severely affected by family disorganization.

In Keith's case, the child had to cope with simple disorganization only. Perhaps this is why the mother responded well to treatment. Although she was antagonistic to her father and her husband, she did have a genuine concern for her son and quite a positive tie to her mother. The latter had seemingly provided her with enough reliable mothering so that she could eventually give to her child without feeling that she was being permanently deprived. Because she relied too much on her own mother, we might say that she was immature and thus not completely ready for the role of homemaker. However, the nucleus of maturity was there and responded to the support and understanding provided by the treatment.

In the case of Paul, on the other hand, the family disorganization was complicated by deep inferiority feelings of the mother. These led to an ambitious need for her husband and son to be successful. Every time they stumbled, her own self-esteem went down. She felt inferior because she had not been basically accepted by her own mother, and had been rejected by her mother as like to her "no-good father." Though treatment continued for two years, little headway was made against these basic limitations in the mother's capacity to mother.

ix

THE TREATMENT

OF LEARNING

DIFFICULTIES IN A

RESIDENTIAL SCHOOL

O UR FINAL case, which will be presented in considerable detail, has several points of difference from the two we have
considered in Chapter VIII. Since the boy to be considered is
ten years old, he is squarely in the middle of the age range of
our original study. More important, his learning problem stems
not from wild expression of uncontrolled impulses, but rather
from a desperate attempt to control his hostile aggression. He
presents the picture of the kind of passive, overly conforming
boy we noted in Chapter VI. As was pointed out there, this
passivity is associated with a chronic low-average score on intelligence tests. Thus, we will not see in this boy the flashes of
bright or superior intellectual functioning we saw in the openly
aggressive pre-schoolers. This boy has a low-average score despite
obviously high educational standards and traditions of his parents.
The educational stimulation from the family is not sufficient to

outweigh the anti-aggressive home atmosphere or to counter-balance his inner resentment toward his ambitious and controlling mother.

However, it is not these facets alone which prompt us to devote an entire chapter to this boy. The learning problem which occasioned the initial seeking of help masked a much more serious personality disorder—so serious that for a time the diagnosis of psychosis was entertained. Because of this disorder, the boy was admitted to the William Healy Residential School where he was treated for about four years. We shall, then, by means of this case, get some idea of the therapeutic milieu of such a school, of how teachers, cottage workers, and therapists attempt to help a boy. We shall see, among other things, that even with the most favorable settings, there still are difficulties in reducing the obstacles to learning.

The Background

The situation began quietly enough. The mother telephoned the clinic wishing to refer her nine-year-old son, Walter, who was having difficulty with his school work and not working up to capacity. She said that he had been tested by a private psychologist who said that Walter's I.Q. was probably higher than the 98 he scored and that his infantile passive and dependent personality was interfering with his school work. Since mother then realized that Walter was at least of average intelligence, she wanted to explore further to see what his problems were. Up to this time, the principal of the school had told the mother that she should not be upset, that she should just go along and see if he wouldn't come out of his problem. However, on the day mother telephoned the clinic, the principal had decided that perhaps Walter needed further help.

The actual report from the school was more ominous than the mother's account:

Walter appears to be living in another world. This is becoming more evident each semester. Very frequently he chuckles and laughs aloud at something which seems to be unrelated to the work going on in the classroom. Occasionally, it is noted that he masturbates—rocking back and forth in his seat, unconscious of his surroundings. He responds and reacts slowly, speaks in a drawling manner, and is immature for his age. This, in part, is probably due to his poor motor control. He is a well-mannered, submissive child and is definitely not a discipline problem. He has little friction with the group because he tends to isolate himself.

Becoming more specific about his school performance, the teacher states:

. . . at present he is barely passing in reading and is failing in spelling, arithmetic, and handwriting. He was held back twice in the past; he was placed in 1-C after one year of kindergarten, since he was not ready for 1-B, and he repeated Grade 3-A. Because of his difficulties, he received remedial reading and tutoring in arithmetic. A primary Mental Abilities Test given at age 5 years 10 months revealed an I.Q. of 83; a Stanford-Binet at 6 years 6 months revealed an I.Q. of 94, and a very recent Kuhlman-Anderson, an I.Q. of 87. In spite of his previous problem in reading, at present he is reading at grade level.

The report by the private psychologist gives a more exact picture of his intellectual functioning. It refers to Walter's behavior during testing:

A nice-looking, pale, somewhat fearful boy who overcame his apprehension rather quickly and came readily to the examination room. At first he was extremely slow-spoken, giving his age incorrectly and mis-spelling his name (and then correcting the errors himself). Here, too, he recovered his poise and for the duration of the test applied himself well, but always worked slowly. More praise and encouragement was required than is considered necessary. With his mother he is very clinging.

Proceeding to the test results, the psychologist states:

The basal age of this nine-year-old boy is at year 6, with a scatter of eight test years, which is very wide. Performance within his test range is also very uneven, thus reflecting a serious fluctuation in his mental functioning. In the field of memory, his performance was most uneven. [For tests at the level of] years 9 and 12, he succeeded in memory for reversed digits, a difficult task requiring close concentration, after having failed similar and easier material at year 7. A similar fluctuation is seen in his verbal facility. Although he was credited for vocabulary at year 10, some of his definitions show infantile selection of a rhyming nature: "puzzle" is a "muzzle," or "haste" is to "hate." There was one bizarre response; when asked for an "animal that rhymes with fair," his response was "rhinocerous." This kind of answer is seen in children at much younger age levels.

The conclusion was as follows.

Present results classify the boy as of average intelligence and they warrant the expectation that as far as intelligence alone is concerned, he could compete with the average of his age in school. However, these results are probably higher than his day-to-day functioning, since they were obtained under ideal testing conditions. At the same time, they are probably lower than his potential. The fluctuation in functioning, the lag in social comprehension, and the infantile and unpredictable verbal selections, all point to disturbing personality factors which, if unchecked, may lead to a serious emotional disorder.

This, then, was the information about Walter which the clinic possessed before the diagnostic interview. Our psychiatric interview with him reinforced the previous impression of his infantilism, passivity, and bizarre responses. Part of this interview report follows:

Walter is a thin, bespectacled nine-year-old boy; he is intense, earnest, yet very childish. He was extremely propitiating and polite. He came willingly with me from the reception room where he was sitting with his mother and father. Along the hall he said, in a very childish way, that it would be a lot of fun playing in the toy room and that the toy room was very nice. This was before he even entered the room. As I was unlocking the door, Walter repeatedly said that he was glad he was going to learn about safety because he thought all little boys should learn about safety. I asked him where he got that idea, and he referred to the safety poster down the hall.

When he came into the playroom, he exclaimed about how nice it was and displayed exaggerated enthusiasm with a politeness that almost verged on mocking. He especially liked the sand box and said that he likes to play with sand, especially on the beach. He said a couple of times that this was a nice room "for a little boy to play in." He referred to himself as a little boy many times during the interview. As he was talking about the sandbox, he said that one must fill the sandbox up because the box may have a leak. He also commented that the sand was very hard, referring to some aggluti-nated clumps of sand that could be fairly easily broken apart, but which were rather hard. Walter's curiosity was very obvious during the whole interview. He looked at everything including my note-book. But he never really explored. He would just take a look at everything that he could see, finger it for a moment or two and mutter the names of the things he was touching and then go on to something else. He muttered to himself throughout the entire inter-view. I could not understand all of what he was saying, but part of the time he was simply telling himself what he saw and what he was doing. For instance, when he explored the toy box and saw a pencil, he said "pencil," "paint box," etc.

Walter was also preoccupied with what was in the sandbox that might be dangerous to him. He seemed to be worried about all sorts of things. I had previously mentioned that he thought the sand was too hard. He found some rusty nails and screws in the sand, and was concerned about them: he took them all out of the sandbox and said, "They're not good for a small boy to play with." He was concerned that there might be glass in there, too, and said that if a boy walks barefoot in the sand, he can hurt his foot on the glass.

When he turned his back to me once, he passed some flatus and said in an exaggerated way, "Excuse me." I questioned him a little more about this, and he said his mother tells him he has to be polite. He said that his "back made a noise," and especially when this hap-pens, as it seems to happen quite frequently, he has to excuse him-self.

In playing with the sand, Walter showed a fair amount of in-genuity in construction. He built a road, and at one end of the road made a garage supported by tongue depressors covered by paper and sand. He put the convertible car in there. Further down the road, in an ambush, was an "armored car." Walter then took the convertible out of the garage, which was driven by a Russian colonel. It came down the road and was stopped by the armored car which came out of ambush and blocked the road. The armored car contained soldiers who were "good guys." The good guys captured the bad Russian colo-nel and the colonel was taken prisoner in the armored car, which went back to the colonel's garage, which was then converted to a jail. One of the good guys "who knows about spy work" took over the colo-nel's convertible, and drove it to a warehouse that contained a lot of weapons and armor. The guy who knew about the spy work threw some bombs in the warehouse and made a quick getaway. The ware-house had enemy arms and was blown up.

Walter then made a bigger load of sand and took the big dump truck to shift the sand around. He was silent, and at this time I asked him why he had come here. Walter answered, "To find the shortest way to school." I asked him if he had any trouble in school and he said that his mother thinks that she should help him in school and he thought he would have to do tests here like he did with the woman psychologist last year. He did not use the word "psychologist." As he was saying this, he found another rusty screw in the sand and removed it "so that the other children won't get hurt."

As he continued to talk about his problems, he always referred to his mother. When he is in school, mother tells him to put up his hand if the work is too hard for him. However, Walter says, this would annoy the teacher, and he didn't want to do it. He goes on to say that the teacher "blows her top" when the kids come at the wrong time. I asked what he meant by "wrong time," and he said he could not answer. I wondered if he meant being late, and he said, yes. I asked Walter if he ever blew his own top, and he said quite seriously and calmly, "Never." However, he did remember blowing his top once when a boy cousin last year broke his plane, which his mother liked very much.

Since very adequate intelligence testing had already been done, a Rorschach test was administered. Here, the bizarreness in behavior and content appeared more ominous:

Walter responded to my introduction of myself with a completely emotionless monologue. During the testing he seemed quite preoccupied with his own thoughts and often grimaced as if some very unpleasant or confusing idea was crossing his mind. Perhaps the most unusual aspect of Walter's reaction to the Rorschach was his literal inability to stop once he started to give responses to a card. Unless I intervened to stop him, he apparently could not prevent himself from continuing to record his ideas ad infinitum. He gave sixty-five responses—even with my limits on his productivity. Only once did he interact with me as a real person. This occurred during the inquiry to Card V. He began daydreaming and looking out of the window until I recalled his attention to our tasks. He incorporated his feeling about this incident into his Rorschach response, which had concerned two men stung by a bee. He now explained, "This bee was disturbed while looking around and it stung both men and they both went nuts."

In interpreting the test results, the psychologist writes:

Walter's Rorschach shows not only a rapid alternation between well and poorly seen precepts, but also between excellent and really bizarre, autistic ideas. Nearly all the classical signs of extreme pathology are present: e. g., "crab with an ink stain on it", "a wolf staring at a wolf's head running away from a fire"; "a woman in her girdle with two spiders on her head"; "the ant tries to squil out of the mud." To sum it up in more everyday language, the Rorschach indicates that Walter is in a very bad state indeed and probably is just managing to stave off a more psychotic break.

Thus, from the diagnostic information so far obtained, the clinic staff became increasingly aware that behind the comparatively mild symptom of a learning difficulty was a severe disintegrative personality disturbance. On the surface, Walter kept himself together by acting like a much younger boy and by extreme passivity and compliance. This apparently was not a sufficient defense, for, at times, bizarre expressions and behavior would break through. Under the placid, conforming surface was boiling rage which, incapable of expression, had its splintering and disintegrative effect on his thought processes.

The staff was naturally very curious about what could be going on in the home to produce such a severe picture. In our account of this aspect, we shall not be as detailed as we have been about the other cases, since our purpose in this chapter is to concentrate as much as possible on what happened within the boy and around him during the four-year period of observation. However, some sketch of the family is necessary in order to understand present and later phenomena.

Walter is the younger of two children, having a sister four years older who is no problem. The family is comfortable financially and above average in economic security and social class. Father is an office manager in a large industrial concern, with 40 employees under his supervision. Not only are he and mother college educated, but on both sides of the family many relatives have been active in education and teaching. Mother has been quite involved with Walter's schoolwork, and she applies discipline around his school problem. She is frustrated at his slowness in school, which she learns of through his papers. For example, the teacher will mark down, "Walter spent forty minutes trying to do five simple arithmetic problems." Her frustration is increased because he does not respond to her threats of eliminating T.V. or forbidding him to play outside with the boys, for Walter is quite content to sit in his room and work on airplanes or read books. He prefers to play with younger boys at childish games such as building dams or manipulating toy trucks.

What aroused the concern of both parents is that neither of them can convince Walter that he should defend himself against other boys, even smaller boys. He has let his cap be taken away and his bicycle damaged. Mother says she could just throttle him for this passivity. When she and father have urged him to stand up and fight sometimes, Walter responds, "But what will the school principal say." In other ways, too, he is extremely attentive to rules of law and order.

Walter's past history is not too unusual except for his having had persistent constipation. This began after an attack of severe diarrhea at the age of one-and-a-half. Mother remembers the diarrhea and its attendant mess and bother as "just awful." We have noted in Chapter VI that constipation was a characteristic symptom in the passive, non-aggressive boys with learning problems. And we saw earlier in this chapter that Walter was particularly apprehensive about the environmental reaction if he passed flatus.

Here, then, in the conflicts about anal excretion do we have the strongest clue as to the origins of Walter's disturbance. Fearful of incurring his mother's displeasure about messy diarrhea, he adopted the strongest safeguard—chronic constipation. All the aggression contained in freedom of the anal sphincter had to be rigidly contained. He could not let himself go in behavior and speed. Yet in his secret fantasies, rockets were exploding and fires breaking out.

The pattern of containing aggression was also prominent in father. His subordinates could not understand how he held his temper, and mother remembered only two occasions in nineteen years in which he had given vent to it. This characteristic was noted in the psychiatric interview with father who apologetically

took most of the blame upon himself. He began the interview
by saying, "I am sorry to have to cause you so much trouble."
When asked his theory about his son's trouble, father said, "I
guess I've been too mean to him." Questioning revealed that by
"mean" father meant that he was rather insistent that his orders
be obeyed.

In contrast to father's self-blame, mother was noted to be
much more blaming and free in her anger. This anger appeared
to be especially intimidating to Walter because several times he
became frightened when he heard mother lecture sister about
an infraction of the rules. Father does say that mother is forceful
around the house and tends to dominate.

With knowledge of the family situation, Walter's problem
became more understandable. Particularly fearful about losing his
mother's love or increasing her wrath, he had inhibited any
aggression that would openly defy her. While one part of mother
had by this time tired of Walter's compliance and wanted him
to be more assertive, the major part of her wanted her men-folk
to be compliant to her domination. The conforming role was
more easily acquired by Walter because he had his passive father
as a model.

The staff's decision about treatment was, of course, based on
the severe personality disorder rather than on the learning problem. Because Walter was considered extremely close to being
psychotic, the staff's recommendation was that he receive intensive, long-term treatment in an institutional setting. The
parents were quite understanding of this decision and eager to
co-operate. Their personality strengths came to the fore as they
began to carry out the recommendations. Mother's own tendency
to blame herself, hitherto concealed, also came to the foreground
at this time. She almost pleaded for therapy for herself, stating
in a manner characteristic of her regard for order, that there
should be a law that every parent whose child is disturbed ought
to be in therapy.

The Institutional Setting

Some description of the institutional setting is necessary. Walter was admitted to the William Healy Residential School, which is a department of the Institute for Juvenile Research. Between twenty and thirty children of both sexes and of various ages live there until they are considered ready to adapt to life outside of the institution. While there, they are physically cared for and looked after by cottage parents, taught for five hours a day by a staff of teachers, and given individual treatment from therapists. In addition to these specifics, there is a general psychological climate fostered, particularly by the director—a climate of benevolence, consistency, and understanding which is designed to correct the pathological family influences to which these sick children have previously been exposed. The children themselves are either definitely psychotic, or, like Walter, are sufficiently withdrawn and autistic that a psychotic break is not unlikely. Because they have to live in cottage groups, somewhat greater preference in admission is given to the passive children like Walter than to the highly impulsive openly aggressive children whose behavior is highly disruptive to group living. In spite of the severity of their emotional disturbances, not all of these children have learning problems. Just as we found in the general admissions to the Institute for Juvenile Research, here also are learners and non-learners.

By virtue of the intimate, day-by-day contact possible in a residential school, we shall be able to follow Walter's clinical course much better than we could if he were an out-patient coming in for weekly interviews. We shall see more graphically how Walter's problem with aggression interfered with his intellectual functioning—particularly in the area of arithmetic.

The Residential School Experience

The first notes on Walter, two weeks after admission, indicate that simple removal from his home has produced no noticeable change in his non-aggressive mode of life. The cottage parent writes:

Walter wanted to call his mother and was permitted to do so. He still asks things in a timid way. "Do you suppose that . . . ?" He reports on the "bad" behavior of other boys, "You'd better tell Frankie not to fool with the record player. He's getting bad." Timidity is also shown in his reluctance to try new foods and in his inability to defend himself against other boys.

Two months later, the report from the teacher indicates that aggressive behavior is becoming less threatening to Walter. She writes:

Until the last week, Walter has remained apart from the other children when they have become upset or run in and out of the room. But yesterday when I had to be unusually firm in keeping order, Walter became very angry with me. In addition to verbal accusations, he threw a book across the room and ran out.

A more quiet and adaptive use of aggression was noted four weeks later by the school teacher:

Walter is completing his written work more quickly and resorting much less often to daydreaming and fantasies. On Wednesday, he tested my reaction to his refusal to do an arithmetic assignment. When I made no issue of it, the next day he did it of his own accord. He holds his own with the other boys now. Twice when Frankie burst into the group and disrupted the class, it was Walter who got up to go after him and stop him. He told Frankie once that he would knock his block off if he did not stop bothering him. Frankie stopped. Regarding his school work, when no pressure is applied by me to do the required task, and when I suggest instead that he pick out what he is interested in, Walter always chooses something at least two years below his present level of functioning.

From the foregoing, we can see that in the first few months at Healy School, Walter made progress. He became much less afraid that his aggression would boomerang. This fear, quite pronounced at home with his parents (and in particular within his relationship with his mother) had made him inhibit his aggression and withdraw into a rage-splintered inner life. In the school he has found no frightening reprisals for being aggressive or stubborn. Although he was no longer as fearful about being his present self, this "self" was not especially zestful about advancing in terms of learning and autonomy, for, when allowed to show spontaneous preference in learning tasks, he selected those below his functioning capacity.

One year after admission, Walter was oriented toward passive comfort and away from the ambitious tensions of adult life; this was evident in the teacher's report:

Walter has been doing the assignments made each day, asking for help when necessary, and finishing in time to have ten to fifteen minutes just to look at library books. The results of the achievement test were one to four years below the level expected for his chronological age. The reading scores were better than the others. He has, on separate occasions initiated discussions with me about what he wants to do when he grows up: he says he wants to be a bum and "not have money worries," to be a building wrecker, or to be an auto wrecker. In these plans of his, it is apparent that freedom from tense responsibility is coupled with a way of ventilating his "aggressive, wrecking" impulses.

Two months later, the impulse indicated in "building and auto wrecking" became manifest in his attitude toward arithmetic, the subject he disliked most. The teacher wrote:

In the operation of "carrying," he asked, "Which gets destroyed, the one or the six?" In long division, he calls the answer "a bomb," and the numbers in the work below are "in the bomb shelter." When he has completed a paper he says, "Now it is killed." The relation of this aggression in arithmetic to his family life could be seen in his statement, "I used to get beatings and drillings from my mother in arithmetic. She tried to beat the numbers into my head. Every time I have to multiply by five, I think of those times with my mother."

One and a half years after admission, the school noted that Walter had relapsed into more withdrawn, non-aggressive behavior. Although various factors could have accounted for this, an important one seemed to have been a change in teachers. While his previous teacher was quite understanding of his need to be openly aggressive at times, the new teacher was less comfortable with such aggression. Her notes read:

Walter continues to get along with adults and children alike. He shuns Andy's bullying. He appears to cry at times. When he is bullied, I reassure him with praise and ego-building. I do not encourage him to fight back physically.

A month later the same teacher wrote:

Walter is no aggressive problem. He's quite afraid when bullied by Andy. I reassure him but do not encourage him to fight back physically. He's less vigorous in his studying, prefers one assignment a day, avoids arithmetic, and his recall is very poor.

The relapse lasted only a number of months. Contributing to its cessation was the understanding of Walter's needs which his new teacher gained through staff conferences. Also important was the growth that the boy had already achieved. It should be emphasized that this kind of relapse is to be expected occasionally in any kind of treatment, be it in a residential setting or an out-patient one. The relapse does not require an outside stimulus; it is a characteristic of emotional growth that after two steps forward there is usually one step back.

The residential treatment review conference two years after admission recognized that Walter was moving forward again though he was still dependent:

The cottage parents report that Walter has again become more aggressive, defends himself more appropriately, and is sticking up for his rights and himself. He is willing, now and then, to fight back when provoked. He still is dependent, as evidenced by his anxiety over the recent illness of the cottage mother. When his therapist left the institution, Walter withdrew into fantasy for a month.

The last two years of his stay were characterized by dependency problems, by conflicts about growing up. As with all the children in a residential school (and with most young people in any school), the nearer Walter came to moving out into a less protected life environment, the more misgivings he had about his ability to cope with it. The more adequately he adapted within the school, the greater was the likelihood that he would be told that he was ready to go back to his family and the public school system. Thus, toward the end of his stay at the Healy School, he, like the other children, showed a slowing up of progress.

Thus, in the beginning of the third year, when Walter was twelve, he began to ask questions about the draft age and how to dodge the draft. He thought "marriage" had many complications because "you don't want to have that old nagging wife." Somewhat later, he claimed the dependent refuge to which psychologically sick people are entitled in his reaction to a cottage father's use of disciplinary firmness: "You look like a hot head, Mr. [X]. I mean, when you get mad, man, you really blow, you know. What's the matter, anyhow, [X], don't you know we're sick boys, I mean, man, really mentally ill, and you can't put us in our rooms everytime we make a boo boo."

Walter's worry about the outside world stemmed largely from the aggression he projected into it. Thus, one year before discharge, he was found reading a book entitled, *How to Protect Yourself in an Atomic Attack*. He said, "You never know what's going to happen in the future, especially this summer."

Although many facets of Walter's treatment and progress are of interest, we shall focus upon the learning area. A picture of Walter's last two years is given in the school progress reports. The first one states:

Walter has been on an academic plateau for most of the past four months and has shown regression. He does little work unless a teacher is at his side helping him at every step. He is "counting up" all his arithmetic even though he has previously demonstrated that he knows the facts about basic addition, subtraction, and multiplication. He has been observed recently mumbling to his work and "bombing" numbers again. However, in the area of reading, he has moved steadily ahead. He is reading two years over his age level.

Six months later the report says:

In the last three months Walter has shown increasing scholastic achievement. He varies greatly from day to day in both the amount of time he takes to complete the assignments and in the amount of real learning he does. The level of work he is doing extends from fourth grade spelling and arithmetic to seventh grade reading. He says he does not want to achieve because accomplishing a task successfully will only mean harder assignments in the future, success will mean that he will be in danger of being sent to public school, and learning in school will eventually mean having to face the world as an adult and either being drafted or having to work to earn money.

Again, six months later:

Walter has shown more progress in his spelling and arithmetic. Particularly favorable results have been obtained in spelling following tachistoscopic work. He will be transferred to part-time attendance at the public school.

The report six months later tells of his experience in public school:

Walter adjusted slowly at [X] school, and, though he showed growth and began doing some of the required written work, he did not complete enough to be graded. The [X] school requested full-time attendance, and he has been so enrolled for the past two months. During this time, he has been able to do all the work except arithmetic; in this subject, he has returned to previous behavior. He has handed in no homework and "just sits daydreaming" in class. Walter has maintained a close relationship with the male teacher at Healy who helped him with his spelling and arithmetic. At the rate he is going, he will probably fail in all subjects.

Subsequently, Walter returned to the Healy School program where he stayed a final six months. The discharge note by the Healy School principal succinctly summarizes his movement in learning:

Academically, Walter's progress was uneven. He made average progress in reading, completing about four years' work in this subject. His progress in science and social studies was also adequate when assignments in these subjects did not require written work. His passive-resistant attitude toward arithmetic, spelling, and completing written work was difficult to break through, and achievement was erratic. At the time of discharge, he was able to achieve at about the sixth grade level in these subject areas, and was able to read and comprehend eighth grade materials with ease.

We could say, in summarizing Walter's entire case, that, while the learning problem was seemingly refractory to treatment, his general emotional problem showed much improvement. Entering the residential home at the age of 10 on the verge of a psychotic break, he left at the age of 14 with much better integration. The original fear of aggressive release which had splintered his thinking and produced bizarre ideas, now was considerably lessened. Fears and anxiety, however, were not eliminated. As we saw, he continued to be anxious about his prospects as a responsible adult.

It was this particular anxiety which blocked him from making consistent academic progress. His teachers had no doubt that he had learned the basics of arithmetic and spelling, but to Walter, a diploma in these subjects was very much like a death warrant. For him it would mean leaving a comfortable familiar place for an anxiety-producing, unfamiliar one. Even pressure about these subjects was comfortably familiar in that it was reminiscent of the nagging and drilling he received from his mother. Finally, he could still use academic failure as a familiar and safe way of thwarting adults.

In terms of learning, then, one may say that Walter's original problem was severe and derived mainly from unconscious anxiety and rage. He experienced so much disintegrative inner turmoil that he could not learn even if he wanted to. His later learning problem was milder and had many conscious components. He was now aware of his anxiety and his resentment. But in his more conscious calculations, he had decided that it was not safe enough yet to put into application what he had learned. It is too soon after discharge to know what Walter will eventually do in the academic area. The fact, however, that his behavior is more influenced by conscious than by unconscious motives makes the prognosis better.

We have presented Walter's case in detail to illustrate a number of points—the relation of inhibited aggression to learning problems (in this case, a blocking in arithmetic rather than in reading), the effect of a family background consisting of an ambitious, dominant mother and an inhibited, self-blaming father, and the dependent immature orientation of the last-born child. The principal new point of the chapter concerns what may happen in a residential academic program. We use "may happen" advisedly because the educational results depend on the individual child. We could have selected other cases in which a dramatic change from non-reading to reading is shown, but we intentionally chose a case which would illustrate the chronic obstacles confronting the teacher.

Children like Walter are not necessarily typical, but neither are they atypical. They test the patience and skill even of teachers who are trained and experienced in dealing with severely disturbed children. If there is a practical lesson to be learned here, it might be that an educator must frequently be content with small, gradual gains.

Part Three

CONCLUSIONS

x

SUMMARY AND

THEORETICAL ASPECTS

*W*HAT, in essence, has this survey of learning problems revealed? And how do these findings fit in with what is generally known about the learning process? These summarizing and integrating questions will command our attention in the present chapter.

In reviewing the highlights of the previous sections, we will recall that the study began with an inquiry into those psychological factors which are specific to learning difficulties. One hundred emotionally disturbed boys with learning problems were compared with 100 emotionally disturbed boys without learning problems. We hoped, for example, to find why a boy with an I.Q. of 110 would be failing in all subjects whereas another emotionally disturbed boy with the same I.Q. would have no trouble in school. Our task was complicated by the fact that learning difficulties did not take one particular form. Thus, among the non-learner boys we saw such different symptoms as lack of motivation, low-average intelligence, difficulties in concentrating, repeating of grades, resistance to the educator, specific difficulty in reading, etc. We turned our attention, then, to finding which emotional or psychological factors are related to the several symptoms of learning difficulties.

Summary of Factors Inhibiting Learning

In general, the factors are: socio-economic status; family disorganization; ambitiousness of parents (especially of the mother); expectations of maturity; and aggression and submission.

Socio-economic Status.—A significantly greater proportion of boys from lower-middle-class or lower-class families were present in the non-learner group than in the learner group. The particular manifestations seen in the non-learner boys from low status homes were: (a) low average intelligence; (b) teachers' descriptions of "dull but working to capacity"; (c) the repeating of grades. These manifestations were explained by lack of motivation in the lower-class family to learn for the sake of learning, by lack of stimulation of the boy's intellect, and by the family's low anxiety about the boy's repeating a grade.

Family Disorganization.—The disorganization of the family was measured by two factors—the incompatibility of the marriage and the employment of the mother outside the home. The non-learners differed from the learners significantly in that many more of the former were from homes in which both factors were present. This was especially true of boys under the age of ten. The particular manifestations seen in the non-learners which appeared to result from this factor were: (a) difficulties in concentrating; (b) reading problems; (c) the repeating of grades. These manifestations were attributed to a chronic feeling of anxious insecurity in the boy as to whether his home would stay intact or come apart. This feeling, in turn, was traced to the personality of the mother who was unable to function as a homemaker or rejected that role.

Parental Ambitiousness.—The effects of this factor were more complicated than were those of the previous factors. In the non-learner group, the mothers were ambitious for the boys with low

average intelligence; whereas in the learner group, the mothers
were ambitious for the boys with superior intelligence. Thus, the
most pronounced learning difficulties were seen in the non-
learner boys who apparently did not have the intellectual capacity to gratify their mothers' need for achievement and status.
The particular manifestation seen was resistance to the teacher,
a resistance which frequently took the form of dawdling or procrastination. Several explanations of this were offered: (1) the
boy can punish his pressuring mother by thwarting her; (2) he
resists the educator in order to preserve his autonomy; (3) he
is afraid of being measured and found wanting; (4) he is afraid
of being measured and found to be successful—since his success
is a threat to his rivalrous mother or father.

Birth Order and Expectations of Maturity.—The non-learner
group had significantly more last-born and fewer first-born sons
than the learner group. To explain this, evidence was presented
that indicated that the last-born tended to be less serious and
responsible than the first born; consequently, the former are less
prone to apply themselves arduously to the task of learning.
Further, it appeared that parents usually have lower expectations of maturity of last-born children than of first-born children.

Aggression and Submission.—In this part of the study, two
aspects of the problem of aggressive behavior were investigated.
First, it was found that parents who did not take responsibility
for their own mistakes, but rather projected the blame onto scapegoats such as their spouses or the schools, tended to have sons
who emulated them in not taking any responsiblity for their own
aggressive behavior. On the other hand, parents who guiltily
took on too much self-blame tended to have sons who were
overly co-operative, submissive, or anxious to please.

The other aspect of the topic dealt with learning itself. The
non-learner group, in comparison to the learner group, more
often showed extremes in the area of aggression; they were aggressively hostile or extremely submissive. In the non-learner

group, both of these extremes were associated with difficulties in reading. The explanation appeared to be that extremes of rage (or anxiety over expressing rage) interferred with learning in general and with the delicate mechanism involved in reading in particular. That the intelligence scores of the openly aggressive boys were higher than those of the submissive ones suggested that the energy of free aggressiveness is necessary for intellectual vigor and alertness.

Other.—The clinical material for young college men and young school boys who were not in the original study of learners and non-learners was presented to augment understanding of the factors we had noted. The essential point was that certain factors played a more significant role in mild college-failure problems, while other factors figured more prominently in more severe primary grade failure problems. Thus, unwholesome parental ambivalence and unrealistic expectations of maturity were more often part of the backgrounds of men who became college failures; while severe family disorganization was more frequently a factor in those children whose primary grade functioning was so handicapped that, for all practical purposes, they were operating as mental defectives.

These, in terse form, are the essential points of the previous chapters. One conclusion is easily evident: namely, that since learning problems have several causes rather than just one, each case has to be understood in its own terms. Understanding why a lower-class boy does not learn will not necessarily help one to comprehend why an upper-class boy fails. Even upper-class boys have different reasons for learning problems—worry about a disorganized family in one case, resistance to an unusually ambitious mother in another. Any one of the factors discussed *may* predispose a boy to some difficulty in learning. The greater the number of factors existing simultaneously in one case, the greater is the likelihood that a learning problem will be present.

Learning Theory

and the Findings of This Study

In relating our findings to what is already known about learning, we are forced to be quite selective. So much has been written from so many viewpoints that a complete survey of the literature would be much beyond the scope and intent of this book. Therefore, we shall limit ourselves principally to the author's area of experience, to what psychiatrists and psychoanalysts have said about learning problems. However, such problems cannot be divorced from what happens in normal learning. For this reason, we must indicate at least some of the noteworthy contributions of psychologists. Though our intention is only to give a general understanding of the issues involved, certain technical articles will be mentioned for those readers who are interested in more specific matters.

The nature of learning has been approached in two different ways. One is concerned with the question of how and why we learn. The principal investigators of this question have been experimental psychologists, such as Thorndike, Hull, and Skinner, who have worked mainly with normal subjects, animal and human. They assume that the learning apparatus is not damaged and that the subject has no marked aversion to learning itself. On this assumption, they have endeavored to find those conditions under which learning is best accomplished. For example, in a hypothetical study of a dog learning to walk on its hind legs, they would point out, among other things, that the dog must have enough motivation or incentive to try to learn the trick and that the trick itself must be within his capacity (no matter how great the incentive, he could not learn to fly).

The other approach to learning centers around the question of how and why we do *not* learn. The principal investigators of this question have been clinical psychologists, psychiatrists, and psychoanalysts. They have worked predominantly with abnormal subjects, who are, for the most part, children with learning problems. Again, they assume that no matter how favorable the setting of the learning situation (in terms, for example, of incentive and capacity), something is interfering with the inner learning mechanisms and is preventing satisfactory learning. They might say, for example, that the reason for a reading problem in a child with good vision and intelligence is that great inner anxiety is overwhelming the integrative psychic mechanisms concerned with reading.

The two approaches we have described are not strictly opposed. They represent, rather, a division of labor. And it should be mentioned that their studies overlap considerably. Experimental psychologists like Maier and Liddell have, by posing impossible learning tasks for rats and goats, succeeded in making them strongly averse to any kind of learning experience. On the other side of the fence, Massermann, a psychoanalyst, has studied a similar phenomenon in cats. Furthermore, such psychoanalysts as Kris, Hartmann, Rapaport, and Kubie have concerned themselves with the more normal aspects of learning and creativity.

Our purpose in presenting this brief "Who's Who" is to give some idea of the different approaches to the problem of learning. This is important because of the frequency with which one hears what seem to be different answers to the same question. These answers are not essentially opposed but rather reflect the different instruments and theories used by the investigators. A psychologist observing how many trials a rat must make before it can run a maze without error will have a different notion of the learning process than will a psychologist who studies the Rorschach responses of a child or a psychiatrist who observes the child in free play.

The Pleasure-Pain Principle in Learning.—What, though, do these observers and theorizers believe in common? Hilgard, in his comprehensive review of current learning theories,[13] lists a number of points about which he thinks most theorists would agree. For our purposes, the general agreement Hilgard cites about the role of motivation is especially pertinent. All agree that learning proceeds best when the subject is motivated to learn a particular skill or knowledge. Furthermore, motivation can be of two kinds: (1) to obtain a pleasurable reward or (2) to avoid pain. Thus, a person can learn to seek a pleasurable situation and can learn to avoid a painful one.

The pertinence of this to our findings is that education can be learned to be sought as pleasure-giving or to be avoided as pain-inflicting. Ordinarily we would say that a boy who dislikes and avoids school has not been successful in learning. But in reality, he has successfully learned that school is painful and should be avoided. It is, of course, more customary to think of learning from the positive viewpoint. Just as a hungry rat learns to push a lever to get food, so a child learns arithmetic in order to retain the love of his parents and teachers. However, just as a rat learns to avoid a certain path in the maze because he receives an electric shock, so might a child learn to avoid arithmetic because he remembers the pain of humiliating embarrassment when he has given wrong answers.

This negative type of learning accounts for some of the learning problems we encountered in the previous chapters. In particular, those problems arising from lower-class status may be viewed in this way. As was said earlier, the lower-class boy frequently does not find abstract education to be positively meaningful, and, often because of painful lack of rapport with the middle-class school system, he may find it negatively meaningful. Thus he avoids education and drops out of school.

In a less direct way, other family factors may have a similar negative learning effect. The learning situation becomes painful when the boy is subjected to relentless harassment at home from an ambitious mother or father who insists he achieve at levels higher than his capability. Though he may not be able to decrease the harassment, he can learn to reduce the pain by not caring whether he succeeds or fails—by ceasing to take learning seriously. In the case of excessively low maturity expectations, the boy has learned that he receives more affection from his parents when he does not grow up, become educated, or assume responsibility. Further, in the matter of too little aggression, the boy has come to find that he gets into much less trouble if he is submissive and non-inquisitive.

To put the matter bluntly, this motivation towards pleasure and away from pain is powerful enough that, given the capacity, organisms can learn to seek or to avoid almost anything. The experimental psychologists beginning with Pavlov have vividly shown this to be true in their prodigious investigations. Their evidence is clear-cut because it relies on the tangible behavior of the animal subjects. Either the rat runs the maze or he does not; either the dog secretes saliva at the sound of the conditioned stimulus or he does not.

The situation in psychoanalysis is more complex. Dealing with such human intangibles as thoughts, fantasies, and feelings, the psychoanalysts cannot hope to come up with as visible evidence as that of the animal experimentalist. Yet the role of pleasure and pain in influencing behavior is paramount in Freud's theories. The technical term "inhibition" refers to a learning problem arising out of a wish to avoid pain. As Freud described it, the ego, in order to avoid painful anxiety, limits its scope of adaptation. It no longer deals with the painful area; it sacrifices a broad adaptiveness for the comfort of a narrow, inhibited scope.[14]

While ego inhibition refers mainly to a general avoidance of painful, anxiety-producing learning situations, psychoanalysts have been much more specific. Noteworthy in this connection is Pearson's exhaustive listing of the various types of learning problems.[15] Perhaps the greatest specificity has been reached in the psychoanalytic theory of reading problems. It deals with psychic components that are most easily observable in children undergoing prolonged treatment. Because the present study of non-learners was based on diagnostic rather than treatment observations, we have not given these components any attention in this book. For the sake of completeness, however, we shall give them a brief consideration here.

Psychoanalytic Theory of Reading Problems.—Most important in reading problems are oral and visual factors. As Freud pointed out, the bodily functions of the mouth in taking things in and of the eye in perceiving things contribute to the first stages of learning. They function normally and in a subordinate fashion as long as the integrating ego is functioning well. However, when the ego is impaired, crude, hostile, and sexual fantasies arise and invade, as it were, the functions of the mouth and the eye. Thus, as Abraham,[16] Strachey,[17] and other have described, the *reading* of words is equated psychologically with the *devouring* of words. Each word may be considered the enemy that is being bitten up and that may bite the reader in retaliation. Consequently, reading is avoided. Something similar is true of the eye. Looking can become sadistic—as in "Looks that can kill"—and the child thus becomes afraid to look in learning. Looking can also be involved in forbidden sexual curiosity and placed under inhibition for this reason. Jarvis and Rosen have been especially interested in the emotional and psychological role of vision in producing reading disabilities.[18]

So far we have been concerned with the role of pleasure-pain motivation in learning, and we have seen that a person can learn to avoid learning. Though it seems paradoxical, we are forced to say that in negative learning there is nothing radically wrong with the learning process. The person has merely learned the wrong things. Though he might be shortsighted in terms of the long range gains and losses, over the short range, he has learned a successful way to avoid painful feelings. He may not be able to read or to do arithmetic, but he is comfortable and can direct his energies into other areas of adaptive learning.

Anxiety, the Ego, and Learning.—In contrast to the previously cited situation is one in which there is an interference with the actual learning process. In this case, the person is relatively incapable of even negative learning. Pleasure and pain do not give sharp signals so that he can consistently seek or avoid them. Instead, there is a diffuse anxiety or rage which renders any learning temporarily impossible. Hilgard mentions this state in connection with motivation: "Motivation which is too intense (especially from fear and anxiety) may be accompanied by distracting emotional states (interfering with tasks involving difficult discrimination)."[19] Accompanying intense emotions is a breakdown of recently learned behavior and a consequent regression to more primitive ways of coping with the world. A familiar example of this is the deterioration in the behavior of a civilized man who is caught up in the violent emotions of a mob.

The effects of strong emotion upon learning was especially noted in the chapters on family disorganization and aggression. The boy who is acutely anxious about his security because his parents are battling and his mother is not home cannot summon up enough energy to learn. As Hilgard says, the distracting emotional state interferes with the ability to discriminate. Similarly, the boy who is filled with rage—that he either expresses or represses in fear of retaliation—is too distracted to tend to the task of learning new things. We may recall that the effects of severe family disorganization were noted especially in boys in the primary grades, where the mastery of the tool subjects is so important. Moreover, extremes of aggression or submission were particularly characteristic of the non-learners. Thus, violent distracting emotions strike directly at the heart of the learning process.

These effects have been noted by both animal psychologists and psychoanalysts. The former have produced experimental neuroses in animals by exposing them to a very difficult task of discriminating between two alternatives. First, they are rewarded by food if they act upon seeing a square and are punished with shock if they act upon seeing a circle. The animals cope with the situation successfully as long as the square remains a square and the circle a circle. But if the square is gradually changed to approach the shape of a circle, the animals are in a quandary. They can no longer tell when they will be rewarded or punished. Filled with anxiety, they tremble and cower, performing erratic, meaningless actions in a stereotyped way. Their ability to use positive and negative motivations, to consistently seek or avoid, has been damaged.

Psychoanalysts have seen similar damaging effects in children exposed to conditions not unlike those to which the animals were subjected. These result mainly from disorganized homes and highly disorganized mothers. The impact is on the small child's ego, the part of the psyche which has the function of perceiving, discriminating, connecting, and deciding. The ego works best when it handles small amounts of stimulation. If it is flooded with excessive stimulation, its functions become severely crippled.

Most psychoanalytic theorists and clinicians are highly impressed by the unifying role that the mother plays in helping the ego develop into a well-functioning integrating mechanism. When she is disorganized and bombards her child with excessive tension, his ego fails to develop properly. Spitz has stressed how impoverished the ego can become as a result of emotional deprivation in infancy.[20] Beata Rank describes a similar state of affairs: "When a mother herself is a poorly organized personality . . . the child's ego remains largely undeveloped and hence is not capable of organizing and controlling drives."[21] Pathological aggression, which as we have noted, plays a most significant role in learning problems, is one of the most frequent signs of a poorly developed ego. Thus, Anna Freud writes that such aggression occurs mostly in "children who are orphaned or grew up in broken homes."[22] Ernst Kris states that the control or neutralization of aggression "does not become effective in institutionalized children because a central love object is absent."[23]

The weak ego resulting from family disorganization is also believed to play a role in reading problems. We have already mentioned the specific psychoanalytic theory—that the child is afraid that the words will bite him in retaliation for his impulse to bite and devour them. The non-specific theory is that excessive disorganization in the mother leads to a weak disorganized ego in the child which prevents him from making the symbolic connections involved in reading. In an earlier chapter we noted that reading problems were frequently encountered when the homes were characterized by marital discord and the absence of the working mother. This is largely in accord with Helen Robinson's findings.[24] Fabian's remarks should also be mentioned in this connection. He believes that reading problems are due more often to a general ego disability that arises from a disorganized home than from one that arises from a specific conflict. He mentions a report by Cunningham of "an unusual incident which developed accidentally in a mill town during the war when mothers were pressed into factory work. Their five-year-olds who could not be accommodated into kindergarten were admitted directly to the first grade. An outbreak of reading difficulties developed in these children as they advanced to the upper grades."[25]

Another note on the role of the mother in the child's learning comes from psychologist O. H. Mowrer, who has been interested in how birds can be taught to speak. He says:

Ideally a prospective [bird] talker should spend several hours of each day in the exclusive company of his trainer. It is commonly agreed among bird fanciers that if you want to teach a bird to talk you must, in effect, behave toward it like a good mother.[26]

Finally, a pertinent observation by Harlow merits mention. In studying how curiosity develops in monkeys he found that:

Contact, nursing and fear are the response systems binding the baby to the mother, and we believe that curiosity represents the primary system releasing the baby from the mother. . . . However, before the infant will leave the mother, the curiosity response must become strong enough to override the fear response, and the mother must not block the infant's exploratory efforts, or on the positive side, the real mother may encourage them.[27]

In other words, Harlow believes the infant monkey must have enough affectional security from the mother before he can satisfy his curiosity by exploratory learning.

Thus, though the mechanics are still obscure, most clinical and experimental evidence points to the mother or mother-figure as strongly influential in determining whether the child's ego will be strong or weak. When she is reliably present and maturely organized, the chances are much greater that the child's ego will be strong enough to integrate and utilize his impulses. If she is absent, unpredictable, or poorly organized, the likelihood is increased that the child's ego will be too weak to tolerate frustration or anxiety and thus will be overwhelmed by crude impulses. Similar conclusions were reached by the present author in a study of normal children and their mothers.[28] These children of eight and nine were in that phase of their development in which academic and social learning was their principal task. It was found that the best adjusted of these normal children had the most emotionally mature mothers and that the least adjusted of them had the least mature mothers.

The foregoing represents our attempts to bring the essential findings of this study into relation with contemporary thinking about learning and its vicissitudes. We have sought to indicate the main areas of agreement between the several schools of thought and the several methods of investigation—rather than the areas of disagreement. Thus, it appears that psychologists and psychoanalysts are in agreement that there are two kinds of learning problems. In one, though the learning process is not grossly damaged, the boy may be motivated by pleasure or pain to avoid academic learning. Due to specific conflicts which produce painful anxiety, he has learned to avoid the educational process and thus remain comfortable. In the other, the learning process is grossly damaged due to a chronic or acute strong emotion which swamps the ego. Though the cause of this ego disability is less specific, it frequently results from the child's being handled by a poorly organized, emotionally depriving mother. This is why we stated in the opening chapter that we have concentrated on the mothers because their role as principal homemaker and first educator is extremely significant in the child's learning.

Learning Problems in Girls

Of the several questions upon which we have not touched, an important one is why boys are more susceptible to learning problems than girls. No definite answer can be given here since girls were not included in the study. But the author's impression, based on his own experience and that of others, is that girls are affected by the same specific and non-specific factors as are boys. Their lower susceptibility to learning difficulties may be due to a less severe dosage of adverse factors or to a greater inner resistance to them. Certainly fewer demands are placed on girls to achieve in school and in life; their self-esteem (and that of their mothers) is not really jolted if they do not become brilliant students. The role of aggression is most likely significant. The naturally aggressive boy is more frequently a problem to mothers and teachers who cannot as easily identify with masculine assertiveness as they can with feminine compliance. Not knowing how to handle it, they tend to put restrictions down too tightly and cause the boy to rebel. Finally, it should be mentioned that girls tend to mature more quickly than boys—so that their readiness to assimilate new learning is comparatively greater.

A remaining topic not fully developed or discussed here relates to the effect of birth order upon personality and learning. Though there has been and still is a considerable difference of expert opinion as to what kind of effect birth order has, the topic has survived as an intriguing area for research. A full treatment of the matter would unduly prolong and complicate this chapter. Consequently, the discussion of the birth order concept has been placed in the Appendix.

Conclusions.—From this summary, the reader may believe that most of the questions about learning and learning problems have already been answered. Nothing could be further from the truth. We must emphasize that much more must be known and that no one discipline has a monopoly on the truth or on the methods of discovering it. Each discipline has certain limitations in seeing the whole picture. The experimental psychologists prefer well-controlled, rather exact investigations done with animals; the educational psychologists are most comfortable with normal rather than atypical or abnormal samples; the psychoanalysts tend to limit themselves to clinical material which emerges during a prolonged intensive therapy.

A similar point is well stated by Hilgard. He writes,

While the state of knowledge is not . . . as bad as the parade of points of view makes it out to be, it is still rather unsatisfactory. There are no laws of learning which can be taught with confidence . . . [To know more] it is desirable to keep the approaches flexible and welcome novelty as well as precision.[29]

The final answers, then, are not yet in. But with collaboration and intellectual cross-fertilization between the various disciplines, our chances of finding the answers are much better.

xi

PRACTICAL

IMPLICATIONS

*N*ow THAT our inquiry into the reasons for learning problems is completed, we shall try to indicate in a general way the connection between theory and constructive action.

The most pressing practical question is, of course, what can be done about learning difficulties. However, that question leads in so many directions that we would be better to ask who can do what about learning problems? This form of the question reflects our belief that there should be a rather distinct division of labor between the parent, the educator, and the therapist. Each of these has distinctive skills and experiences; each meets the child in a different setting. Though some overlapping in their functions is inevitable, the majority of their actions should spring from their special understandings and capacities.

The parents can do most good in the *prevention* of learning difficulties. This they can accomplish by fostering a home atmosphere which is conducive to the boy's learning. Above all, they should prevent the young boy who is starting school from being exposed to unusual family disorganization. The combination of marital discord and a working mother has an especially damaging effect on the boy's ability to master the tool subjects in the primary grades.

Ideally, the parents should strive to reduce to a minimum those other factors found to produce learning difficulties. Thus, they should respond positively to the child's intellectual curiosity and reward his learning achievements; they should expect achievement which is consistent with his capacity; they should require of him a maturity which is consistent with his chronological age; they should, by example, instruct him as to his own involvement in transactions with other people; and they should accept and help to channel his healthy aggressions.

The teacher stands midway between the parent and the therapist. Not only does she act so as to *prevent* learning problems from developing, but it is also a part of her function to *remedy* learning difficulties which are in the process of developing. In a preventive way, she strives to create an emotional atmosphere conducive to learning. The same guidelines mentioned just previously in regard to the parents are especially pertinent to her own role. However, because she has quite a number of students in her classroom, she cannot individualize the child as much as the parent can or as much as the therapist can. In addition to her preventive work, she can do a type of first-aid correction of early learning difficulties—through special help, by adjusting pressures, or by conferring with the parents, etc. When the learning problem does not respond to these first-aid measures, she refers the child to a specialized person in the school system (like an adjustment counselor) or to a clinic where psychotherapy or remedial reading is available.

For the therapist, whose function is primarily to *cure* rather than to prevent, the technical details of his work are beyond the scope of this particular book. It may be said, however, that he helps in both general and specific ways. In a general way, he provides the boy with an individual, reliable, realistic, and benevolent atmosphere which reduces the young patient's anxiety and antagonisms and which allows the boy to use his energy for learning. This therapy of the individual relationship is all that some mild learning problems require and is all that some boys with severe learning problems can utilize in the beginning stages of their treatment. Besides this general kind of help, the specific interpretations of the knowledgeable therapist enable the boy to become conscious of what is motivating his behavior. Thus, for example, by therapeutic interpretation, the patient can grow aware that his avoidance of reading is due to a fear that the words will bite back or to a fear that reading is equated with forbidden sexual curiosity.

There is little doubt that learning problems which have failed to respond to the first-aid measures of the teacher and the parents could benefit from individual therapy. Unfortunately, all boys with such problems do not receive treatment. An important reason is a lack of trained therapists. However, frequently it is due to the lack of co-operation by parents who feel that their son would be stigmatized by undergoing therapy. Sometimes, too, the parents do not want to examine their own emotional attitudes toward their son, preferring that he remain infantile or pressured. Sometimes they are impatient for quick how-to-do-it answers, being unprepared or unwilling to invest time and energy in their son's treatment.

Because all learning problems do not receive therapy, it is doubtful whether one can generalize about their nature if one deals only with treated cases. Our study of non-learners was conducted on boys referred by the schools. Only 20 per cent of these, however, were treated. This minority of non-learners included generally boys having middle- or upper-middle-class parents who were interested enough in their son's education that they were motivated to co-operate in his treatment. This trend is in keeping with Redlich's conclusion that psychotherapy is utilized more often by the upper social classes. Besides motivation, the parents (and especially the mothers) tended to recognize that they had contributed in some way to their son's emotional disturbance, rather than claiming it was all the fault of their spouses or of the school. For these reasons, treatment cases of learning problems, though very illuminating, are not completely representative.

This brief sketch of who can do what about learning difficulties does not do full justice to the unique position of the teacher. Her position is not only unique but also somewhat unenviable. She, or the school curriculum, is frequently made the target of attack by parents whose ambitions or short-comings are excessive. Because much has already been written about teachers' having to understand children and parents, we feel it more useful to direct our attention to the other side of the coin— to give parents some understanding of teachers and their roles. By so doing perhaps we can also enable the teacher to be less conflictful about what she is supposed to do.

Within the school setting we may ask, "What can parents realistically expect of the teachers?" and "What can the teacher expect of herself?" The parents cannot expect her to do their job of supplying the child with his basic emotional security. Nor can they expect that the teacher and the ordinary classroom situation will immediately if ever eliminate chronic, severe anti-learning characteristics in the child. They *can* expect the teacher to be skilled in a craft, well-intentioned toward the child, interested in his intellectual growth, and co-operative toward any measures that will benefit him. These last remarks cover essentially what the teacher can expect of herself. In spite of pressures from without or her own wishes from within, it seems best that she should resist being encumbered with or drawn toward the *majority* of duties that properly belong to the parents or to the therapist.

We are certainly not the first to suggest that the teacher leave major therapy to the specialist. Many years ago, Anna Freud, a psychoanalyst, wrote in her *Introducion to Psychoanalysis for Teachers*:

You . . . are in a most advantageous position. An immense amount of material passes through your hands in your daily work and teaches you to recognize very clearly the whole range of phenomena before you; from the physically and mentally retarded children, the obstinate, cowed, lying and ill-treated children to the brutal, aggressive, and delinquent ones . . . but the very situation which gives you such a complete knowledge of the phenomena has its drawbacks. You are obliged . . . ceaselessly to *act*.[30]

Anna Freud goes on to say that because the teacher has to act as an educator, it will be a long time before teachers can utilize psychoanalytic theory in the actual practice of teaching.

Much more recently, Harry Rivlin, an educator participating in a symposium of the American Orthopsychiatric Association on learning problems had this to say,

There are so many significant differences between the ways in which the psychiatrist and teacher view learning that we gain little if the teacher follows procedures that are appropriate for a psychiatrist. . . . No teacher can ever hope to understand an individual child as fully as a psychiatrist does even if the teacher has the necessary training and background. Teachers must learn, therefore, how to work with children whom they will never know as thoroughly as the clinician does. . . . The teacher has a very real responsibility for creating a wholesome emotional climate in which children can develop and learn to adjust to themselves and others. . . . This is where the teacher makes his greatest contribution rather than in amateur attempts at analyzing and treating serious emotional disorders.[31]

Finally, in this connection, we shall quote from Gilbert Highet's charming and enlightening book, *The Art of Teaching*. Though Highet writes as a humanist rather than a scientist (in fact he is "anti-scientific"), his conclusions are almost identical with ours. Second, his ideas about what is the essence of good teaching or the essence of the learning situation support our theoretical conclusions about the importance of a positive reliable involvement of educator with pupil.

Highet gives the qualities of a good teacher: "(1) He must know what he teaches. (2) The second essential is that he must like his subject. (3) The third essential of good teaching is to like the pupils."[32]

There are two powerful instincts which exist in all human beings and which can be used in teaching. These are *gregariousness* and the love of play. . . . We said that one function of the teacher was to make a bridge between youth and maturity. If he has a sense of humor he can build the bridge. The young think their elders are dull. The elders think that young are silly . . . yet a clever teacher who can use her sense of humor in such a way as to show the young that not everyone over 25 is dead, will at the same time learn enough about her pupils to see that their silliness is only awkwardness, easy to penetrate and dissolve. Both sides will understand each other better and work together. Togetherness is the essence of teaching.[33]

To us, Highet's views and suggestions seem very sound. They set positive goals for the teacher which are in keeping with her particular training. It is interesting that from personal teaching experience he reaches conclusions quite similar to those reached by scientific investigations. The only issue we would take with Highet concerns his insistence that teaching is an art, not a science. His view is understandable if his main contact has been with psychological scientists who are interested only in measurable quantities. He then would be justified in saying, "It seems to me very dangerous to apply the aims and methods of science to human beings as individuals."[34] But, as our study has shown, humanism as reflected by the mother-child relationship is an essential part of the science of human behavior; there *is* a scientific basis for humanism. Highet's "You must throw your heart into it, you must realize that it cannot all be done by formula,"[35] is a more direct and eloquent way of stating some of what we have been trying to say in this book.

The foregoing might indicate that our only suggestion to teachers is that their hearts be in the right place. Though this is important, we do not intend to minimize the role of the teachers' minds. As Highet indicated, they should know their subject and continue to learn more about it. But what thinking should they do about their students? Again Highet puts it well. After saying that the teacher must like the pupils, he asks, "Is it also essential to know the pupils?"[36] He concludes that, except for the tutorial system, it is sufficient generally that the teacher get to know types of students rather than each student as an individual.

The art of teaching like the art of healing, consists partly in recognizing in each individual a particular type or combination of types. In ten or fifteen years [the teacher] will assemble a little gallery of types which singly or combined will account for eighty-five per cent of the average class. . . . Some unclassifiable individuals will always remain. . . . These [eccentrics] you must learn to know as individuals.[37]

In this connection, we have tried in the preceding chapters to indicate some *types* of learning problems. Thus, the majority of boys may fall into such group types as the unmotivated and unstimulated lower-social-class student; the anxious, poorly concentrating boy from a disorganized home; or the resistant lad who has been unwisely pressured by his ambitious parents. The chapter on birth order indicated that the first-born and the last-born may differ in personality and thus may need to be handled differently. An excellent description of their divergent characteristics—the first-born's need not to be interfered with and the last-born's comfort in being dependent—is given by Dostoevsky in the *Brothers Karamazov*. (This description will be found in the Appendix B.)

There are, then, types of boys and types of learning problems. Though the teacher frequently has enough to do in learning and teaching her subject, in preserving discipline, and in maintaining her good mood, considerable benefits will accrue to her and to her students if she gradually recognizes the types with which she deals. Though she may not always be able to act upon this insight, nonetheless, as the French say, *comprendre est pardonner* ("to understand is to forgive").

Parental Ambition and General Education

We should like, in the concluding pages, to offer some reflections on how one of our factors—parental ambitiousness—

affects the general educational picture. We have already seen how this pressure is resisted by boys with learning problems and complied with by boys with no learning problems. Moreover, it will be recalled that overly ambitious parents are frequently intolerant of slowness and welcome speed. The pertinence of this to general education is that parents are taking an increasing interest in the schools, and are, through active and sometimes militant P.T.A. groups, having a stronger voice in the school policy. While much of this recent development is desirable, it is necessary to point up some of the dangers involved in an unrealistic and unwholesome speed-up.

As a background statement, it must be acknowledged that general education, rather than learning problems, is the subject which has captured most of the interest of the citizenry. Although they are distressed to learn that there is a sizeable proportion of boys with at least average intellectual endowment who fail to keep pace with their classmates and more distressed by the problem of mental deficiency, they are more actively interested in the education of the non-handicapped. They ask "Given a student who is quite receptive to learning, how can we best help him to realize his full potentialities?" This question is undoubtedly a fair one, and, taken by itself, it deserves a serious consideration which is outside the scope of this book. But the legitimacy of the query is so often clouded by a number of undertones that we are prompted to devote some space to discussing them.

One of the disturbing undertones arises from the understandable wish of parents that their children be in the most advantageous position to cope with future adult life. As the present author pointed out in his study of normal children and their mothers,[38] this wish frequently takes the form of a desire for limitless improvement. Whether this springs from the parent's hope that the child will carry out the parent's unrealized intellectual aspirations, or from the knowledge that it will pay off for the child to have had a college education, a frequent result is that the parents pressure the children and the schools to give their utmost. We have seen in one of the early chapters what a tricky business ambition is—how in some cases the backfire occurs soon enough that a marked learning difficulty is produced in the primary grades and how in other cases is postponed until college. Unless parental ambition is wisely tailored to the child's actual capacities, it can be detrimental.

Since knowledge may be power, and education, the royal road to status, there is indeed more than a grain of truth in parental feelings that education pays off. An interesting example of how these feelings can be disproportionally stimulated is provided by a recent book entitled *How to Raise Your Child's I.Q.* It states,

In school, children are grouped in classes in accordance to their IQ. The curriculum is gauged to the IQ of the whole class. Thus, a single point in your child's score can make the difference between a routine education and the greatly enriched curriculum being taught to classes in the next IQ range.[39]

After pointing out the unwelcome consequences of a "routine education" (poor opportunities in the armed forces and in later job-seeking) the book gives practical suggestions on how the child can be coached before an I.Q. test.

"Enriched Curriculum" as a Manifestation.—How the term "enriched curriculum" originated is not known. But if it was coined by the educators, it may well be that they have opened a veritable Pandora's box. They are placed in an unenviable position similar to that of the hero *Arrowsmith* who, for scientific purposes, had to withhold a wonder drug from one-half of a plague-stricken population. Although the building and revising of curricula are very properly among the functions of the educators, they may be creating a panicked demand for their "enriched" product without having enough trained personnel to supply it. In the face of such a demand, they would be compelled to cut corners, to thin out the educational soup. They would incline toward reducing the personal relationship between

teacher and child and toward increasing impersonal devices such as television. While there is no doubt that television is and will be of some use in education, there is a great danger that, due to the excessive demand, it might be employed indiscriminately. Fortunately, however, some educators have come to realize not only the limitations of television but also the repercussions of overselling their product as "enriched."

"Creativity" for All as a Manifestation.—"Creativity" is another term which promises magical fulfillment for ambitious parents and for some teachers. In the past, it was rather strictly defined and referred to what went on in the minds of indisputably creative people. Currently, however, there is a much looser definition which frequently serves as a catch-all for all activities faintly resembling proven creativity. It is the current loose definition—with all its potentialities for confusion and false hope—with which we shall deal.

Whereas the term "enriched" brings up an image of a student being fattened up with a broad educational diet or energized with educational vitamins, the promise of "creativity" arouses the image of a student becoming a genius. This acts as a lure for certain people with intellectual or artistic leanings. For they often feel more complimented by being called creative than by being called constructive. They would rather hear the teacher say of their child that he shows a creative streak than that he is constructively utilizing his intellectual endowment.

Some educators—especially those in certain private schools—are not immune to the creativity fever. We do not refer to the teachers who facilitate the intellectual growth of the very occasional student who is undoubtedly creative. Rather, we refer to those teachers who feel they have failed unless they have brought out some interesting creative facet in the majority of their students. Even if they are not interested in bringing the majority up to that level, they are not sure that that bored boy with the superior intelligence who is looking out the window might not be a second Edgar Allen Poe or Lord Byron, and consequently they believe that they ought to revise the curriculum to make it more interesting. We found in our study that the inattentive boy who is working below capacity but who has superior intelligence was reacting more to insecurity and parental over-ambitiousness than to an unstimulating curriculum. This is not to deny that occasionally curriculum changes may be very useful in such cases. Our point is simply that some schools have become quite creativity conscious.

Part of the source of this attitude can be attributed to the claims made for psychoanalysis. A popular idea is that if one simply removes the inhibitions, a flowering of creative genius will result. Yet the psychoanalyst Pearson writes:

It [creativity] will be found only in a very few pupils and is the result of certain specific influences in their early lives. . . . Ability in creative art is the result of certain definite intrapsychic conflicts. It simply exists or does not exist; and if it does not exist it cannot be inculcated.[40]

This denial of magical powers by psychoanalysts may be feeble in comparison to what people expect of psychoanalysis and especially in comparison to what people hear about what is being done in the field of science. After all, if science can get a computer to beat a human being at chess, why is it not possible to bring out this same proficiency in a child?

That there is presently a promise of creativity in the air is indicated by the title of a recent book *Creativity and Its Cultivation*.[41] From the title alone one may get the impression that everybody possesses potential creative ability and that all that is necessary for its fruition is its proper cultivation. The contents of the book, which represents the contributions of several writers, however, are much more serious and can serve as the departure point for our discussion.

The most optimistic view—one which holds the promise of creativity for everyone—is given by the educator George Stoddard. He states:

Creativity came close to being a lost cause in American education.

Progressive education, a phenomenon rarely observed in pure form, helped to revive its spirit. . . . The urge to inquire, to invent, to perform was stifled in millions of school children. . . . We may postulate that everybody has some spark that education can blow upon and make brighter.[42]

Stoddard's belief in the possibility of mass creativity certainly puts the educational system in the position of being reproached if every pupil's creative spark cannot be made to burn brighter.

Margaret Mead, an anthropologist, sees, however, limitations to universal creativity. She writes:

Another repercussion of Freudian thinking and of the general educational outlook of the 1920's was the emphasis upon creativity as something natural to childhood which, if only given freedom, would blossom into works of great beauty.[43]

From her experiences with the artistic efforts of South Sea Islanders, she concludes, though, that "It [is] clear that freedom alone was not enough to provide for more than an initial creative effort which then became . . . repetitious."[44] Mead, in essence, is cautioning us not to mistake the first artistic flowerings of children for signs of embryonic genius which needs only further encouragement to cause it to flourish. However noble the intention of democratic equalitarianism that everybody should be equally creative, the facts appear to make this intention Utopian. A critique of this misleading utopianism is supplied by Erich Fromm who wrote in this particular volume:

[In the past] equality meant that we each have the same human dignity in spite of the fact that we are different; it meant the right to develop one's differences. Today, equality means sameness.[45]

Fromm's point about individual differences leads us to a consideration of how indisputably creative work actually gets done. There is a strong body of thought that leans toward the idea that concerted co-operative group action is highly important in solving investigative problems. In this view, individual differences and goals are de-emphasized; all the creative people should pull together toward the solution of the shared task. Henry Eyring suggests this orientation when he states "The Lone Wolf has solved many problems, but an increasing number of scientific enterprises are becoming highly co-operative and require social integration."[46]

The extreme of this view is seen in creative crash programs such as "brainstorming." Here several creative people are brought together and encouraged to say whatever comes to mind about the particular problem. The group interstimulation is supposed to accelerate and improve the quantity and quality of creative thought. Hilgard, however, points out the limitations of this method: "The group process did *not* yield proportionately more ideas, more unique ideas or ideas of higher quality. In fact, it could be supposed that in some way the group process *inhibits* creative thinking." To temper this, Hilgard adds, "The general idea behind brainstorming is to create a mood for free flow of ideas. Once this mood is created, the group process is not essential to its validity."[47]

More generally, Hilgard does not share Eyring's view of the necessity for social integration:

Responsibility, social adjustment, being a good citizen, accepting a conforming role—these have their costs, too. . . . We must not fool ourselves that good social adjustment is the best condition for all human production. . . . We must not develop critical abilities to the point that anything unproven is stupid or that anything weak is altogether wrong. We must not insist upon conformity or we will end with traditionalists rather than with innovators.[48]

The author believes the opinions of Hilgard, Fromm, Mead, and Pearson are more in keeping with the realities of the situation than is Stoddard. Creativity in the strict sense is not within the reach of the majority of students; its increase would depend as much, if not more, on the influences within the family than on stimulation from the formal educational system. On the other hand, a creative, constructive attitude toward life is something that is much more accessible to a larger number of young persons. Though the family influences are important here, too, the efforts of educators can have much more significance.

We should, then, be cautious in following the ambitious lures held out by "creativity" and "enrichment." Our American culture —already enamored of speed and short cuts—does not need the additional stimulation provided by these terms. If we are not on guard, our tempo—conditioned by the instantaneous communication of television and the great velocities of jet planes—might become even more unbearably quick. If the Olympic games can be taken as a guide, we are already specialists in the dashes and the relay races; the Europeans do much better in the distance events. Our fortes, then, are short distances and fragments which can be mastered quickly. We lack the patient endurance needed for the broader, long-range synthesis.

The pertinence of this to our main thesis is that the learning process is characterized by frequent plateaus, by phases of consolidation and integration on which no discernible forward movement is seen. Such plateaus are intolerable to those in our socially mobile culture who are ambitiously driving toward greater status. For them, educational results must occur quickly and visibly. If there were such a thing as "instant learning" they would be the first to embrace it. These people as citizens do have some voice and influence in general educational policy. We believe that this influence should be countered by the educators who are more knowledgeable about the way learning actually takes place.

The matters of proper tempo and integration are prime distinguishing features of living organisms rather than of machines. Organisms require periods of rest, of incubation and gestation, during which fatigue products are eliminated and integration takes place. Machines require much less of this. Yet, as others have pointed out, we are in danger of taking the machine for our life model rather than the organism. It is not just a coincidence that our mechanistic age has also been described as an age of speed, of anxiety, of loss of personal identity, or of fragmentation. To counter these trends, we must reaffirm that no matter how attractively time-saving the jet and the automatic computer may be, it is the mysteriously complex human mind with its own integrating tempo upon which we must place our hopes—and trust that its potentiality for error will be outweighed by that for truth.

APPENDICES

a

METHODOLOGY

Form of the Investigation

*t*HE STUDY we have elaborated was a retrospective, exploratory clinical study conducted by a single investigator for several reasons. Time, energy, and budget are of course important in determining the magnitude of any project, and these factors undoubtedly played a part in making the study retrospective and of an individual rather than team nature. Especially important was the desirability of maintaining a balance between guarding against error and finding illuminating connections. Each approach can be abused; examples are the over precise kinds of studies from which emanate sterile and obvious conclusions and the overly loose kinds from which issue wild flights of ideas. The particular balance struck in this investigation is one that fits the personal equation of the writer. Though we have reported only statistically significant results, we have deliberately included conjecture. Stated in somewhat different terms, some of the mental energy which would have gone into making the study more sophisticated and quantitatively rigorous, went into a speculative qualitative analysis of the data—and vice versa. Though the text is written with a certain emphasis and persuasiveness, the author is keenly aware that conclusions and hypotheses are

[171]

but resting points from which one must go on to make new observations.

Methods of Study

The actual methods derived from the commonly accepted assumption that children with at least average intelligence should be able to do their school work adequately. The next assumption was that if they do not (and if organic and pedagogical factors are excluded) the causative factor is some emotional disturbance in the child and/or the family. In the actual investigation, steps were taken to rule out the factors of below-average-intelligence and organicity. Faulty teaching methods, however, could not be ruled out.

The important point is that once below-average-intelligence was excluded as a factor, intelligence scores were no longer used in differentiating the two groups, learners and non-learners. Thus, while it is true that in the learner group, as compared with the non-learner group, there were considerably more boys with an intelligence quotient of over 110, this was not pertinent to the essential question of the study. The question was not, are the brighter boys less susceptible to learning problems than the duller boys, or are the emotional blocks to learning different in boys with superior intelligence than in boys with average intelligence. It was rather, what are the emotional factors which interfere with learning despite the presence of adequate intelligence. Consequently, efforts were made to discover what there was in common between the obviously failing non-learners and the learners who were not working up to capacity. These assumptions and questions account for the fact that no matching of the two groups was done as to intelligence or age. Whenever, though, these factors appeared to influence the results, they were noted.

The investigation began with a review by the author of consecutive cases seen diagnostically at the Institute for Juvenile

Research beginning with the year 1953. The first step was of a general nature designed to narrow the selection and to improve the quality of the data. The cases had to meet the following specifications: 1) minimum I.Q. of 90 on an individually administered psychometric test; 2) no proven or strongly suggestive organicity; 3) an informative and adequate school report; 4) an informative and adequate social history.

The next step involved the setting up of two groups of: 1) the learners whose causes for referral never included a learning difficulty, who had never repeated a grade, and whose school reports indicated that they were currently doing at least average work; 2) the non-learners whose causes for referral were solely or predominantly learning problems and whose school reports confirmed this complaint (an additional criterion was that they be failing in at least one subject). About 450 consecutive cases closed between 1953 and 1955 were reviewed in order to obtain the two groups of 100 suitable cases each.

After this procedural step, the author read each case thoroughly in the hope of obtaining a holistic formulation of the psychodynamics differentiating the non-learner and learner groups. Little success was forthcoming. In an effort to reduce the complexity of the investigation, the author then abstracted the routinely available clinical information about each of the two hundred cases. Little or no judgment was involved in abstracting the school report which consisted for the most part of multiple choice items checked by the school teacher. The same consideration obtained for that part of the social history which dealt with social class, intactness of the family, employment of mother, number and position of the siblings. Personal judgment did, however, play a role in abstracting the narrative description of the child by the school teacher and such features of the family as marital discord, ambitiousness, maturity expectation, projection of blame, and early developmental problems. Of course, a decision as to what should be abstracted had to be made. Though implicit hypotheses about learning problems undoubtedly influenced the author, the prime consideration was whether information about a certain aspect was available in most of the cases. Thus, every item on the school report and all social history information concerning the current family situation were included. Due to variability of coverage, the childhoods of the parents and the psychiatric examination of the child were not suitable for abstracting.

The abstracted clinical information was then handled statistically. Three different statistics were used in testing the level of significance: 1) where it was important to determine whether specific percentages compared were significantly different, the Z test for the difference between proportions was used; 2) where the problem was whether the total pattern of variation was significantly different, the chi-square test was used; 3) where the sample was broken up into a number of sub-groups each of which was too small to yield significant results, the probability of comparison within each sub-group that replicated another was calculated by the binomial theorem.

All results referred to in the text and found in the tables are, unless otherwise stated, significant at least to the 0.5 level. A few sub-significant trends are also reported. With one exception (the comparison of intelligence scores of co-operative learners and aggressive non-learners), no effort has been made to report negative results. Thus, the lack of significant correlation between learning problems and the attitude of the father and between learning problems and the pressure of an academically achieving sibling, is not reported. We should note, however, that not all of the significant results have been reported. After the data were examined statistically, each case was read again to secure a more holistic impression. In the main, only those results which could be meaningfully integrated by some theoretical structure are presented in the test and tables, and only those theoretical structures for which no contradictory results were found are considered.

By now, it must be abundantly clear to the reader that both qualitative and quantitative methods were used in this investigation, the former being addressed to the whole, the latter to the parts. The combined approach was not accidental. Rather, it stemmed from the author's opinion that sole reliance should not be placed on quantitative, objective methodology. While this method contributes very appreciably to the understanding of the parts, it should be supplemented by more subjective methods if one wishes to approach a fuller understanding of the whole.

b

REVIEW OF

THE BIRTH

ORDER CONCEPT

t HE POTENTIAL importance of birth order rests in the fact that it is one way of accounting for individual differences within the same family. To be sure, hereditary factors and changing family situations play a prominent part in explanations of why a boy learns differently than his brother. But since we have found that the mother is of central importance, we might expect that the different quantities and qualities of maternal attention toward the first-born and the later-born children would have some distinctive repercussion on ego development and learning.

Birth order has had a strange and fascinating history of attention and neglect at the hands of investigators. At present, it is in a phase of decided neglect. It is the purpose here to attempt to correct this imbalance. We do not wish to elevate this factor to a position of unique or maximum importance, nor do we want to make a universal theory of it. Rather, we wish to restore birth order to its proper place of being *a* factor differentiating men and *a* factor worthy of serious consideration.

Before dealing with the interesting history of this concept,

it may be helpful to review the essential points made in Chapter
V. It was found that the *first-born* were more likely to be in the
group of boys *without* learning difficulties, while the *last-born*
were more likely to be among the boys *with* learning difficulties.
This differentiation seemed to issue from personality characteristics of the first- and last-born rather than from differences in
their intellectual endowment.

The personalities of the first-born were characterized by tendencies to be overly serious, identified with the responsibilities of
the parent, and resistant to pressures. On the other hand, the
personalities of the last-born were characterized by tendencies to
be carefree, delightfully charming, needing to win support, and
showing a "looser" inner control—"impulse spilling" was rather
frequent. These trends were believed to issue from the differing
maturity expectations of the parents, the first-born is expected
to be too mature, to be aware of the duties and responsibilities
of life; the last-born is permitted to be insufficiently mature and
to carry out a regressive enjoyment of life.

What was not mentioned in the earlier chapter is that the
first-born children, for better or worse, tend to receive more maternal attention than do later-born children. For the better, it
provides a protection against the various learning difficulties
which derive from the emotional absence of the mother. For the
worse, the maternal anxiety contained in this attention creates
pressures against which the first-born are resistant. While the
later-born tend to escape the full brunt of maternal anxiety, they
do not usually receive as much sustained maternal attention.

Despite the plausibility of these ideas and the easily noted
differences between the first- and last-born, the concept of ordinal
position has not taken hold. This can be demonstrated by con
sulting some books on educational psychology. Such books are
extremely significant because they are the principal books used
in the instruction of teachers, and because their contents represent the most useful insights gained from research in educational
psychology, in learning theory, and in psychoanalysis. Three rep-

resentative books will be mentioned: Cronbach's *Educational Psychology*,[1] Lindgren's *Mental Health and Education*,[2] and Redl and Wattenberg's *Mental Hygiene in Teaching*.[3] Despite the competence of these books, the fact remains that neither Cronbach nor Lindgren make *any* mention of ordinal position; while in Redl and Wattenberg's insightful 445-page book, one page is devoted to ordinal position and one page to the special situation of the only child.

If we go to the main contributors to the field of educational psychology, we find a similar situation existing in learning theory and psychoanalysis. In the last ten or fifteen years, mention of ordinal position has been minimal. Hilgard's review of learning theories makes no mention of it. Since its inception fifteen years ago, there has not been one paper in the fifteen annual volumes of the *Psychoanalytic Study of the Child* which deals specifically with ordinal position. Perusal of the very comprehensive *Psychological Abstracts* reveals a disproportionately low number of articles dealing with this subject in the last ten to fifteen years.

One could properly ask, "Is not this neglect deserved?" "Perhaps," one might say, "ordinal position was a wrong trail or a blind alley. After all, the epicycles devised by Ptolemy to explain the sun's revolving around the earth or the theory that the night air was dangerous were proven erroneous and gave way to a more scientific account of events." This, of course, is always a possibility, but, as the history of interest in this topic will shortly indicate, it is highly improbable.

In the modern history of this idea, the first noteworthy contribution was made by Francis Galton, an anthropologist, in 1874;[4] it was followed by the studies of Havelock Ellis in 1904,[5] Cattell in 1917,[6] and Terman in 1925.[7] The first three authors investigated eminent scientists or other well-known creative individuals. Galton and Cattell found that first-borns were much more frequently found in these eminent groups than were middle- or last-borns. Ellis found a trend in favor of the first-born and last-born. Terman found a preponderance of first-borns in 1,000 intellectually superior children.

After this promising start, what happened to the interest in the relationship of ordinal position to intellectual creativity? One cannot answer with certainty but can form some conjectures. It is not unlikely that the decline was due to the waning of Terman's interest in the matter. In his first volume of *Genetic Studies of Genius*, the trend referred to above was mentioned. In his third volume—which consisted of a follow-up of his 1,000 gifted children, ordinal position is not mentioned as a factor influencing later professional status or choice of profession. In his later monograph, ordinal position is definitely mentioned as *not* significantly influencing choice of profession.

Without Terman's leadership and authority, the topic seems to have fallen into comparative oblivion in psychological circles. Also there was no impetus from the experimental workers in learning theory who studied animals. Since most of the experiments were done with rats, there would have been no opportunity to deal with ordinal position. In a litter of rats, the first- last-born are not distinguished. Rather, they are observed with relation to their weight, age, heredity, whether they had ever encountered the maze before, etc. With little or no stimulation from the experimental psychologists, then, the import of ordinal position dwindled. In this connection we quote from H. Jones, writing in the *Manual of Child Psychology*.

In an earlier critique (Jones 1933) of research in this field, evidence has been given that when . . . methodological difficulties are properly controlled . . . no birth order differences in intelligence occur in normal samples. . . . Atypical results, however, have been encountered in certain highly selected samples. . . . Studies of gifted children by Terman (1925) and of eminent men by Ellis, Cattell, and Huntington have shown a distribution of birth order differing from chance expectation and strongly favoring the first-born. . . . No satisfactory explanation of this finding has been given.[8]

A similar decline in the interest in ordinal position can be seen in social psychology, the branch of psychology whose experimental subjects are mainly humans rather than animals. A promising start was supplied by Miller in the early 1930's when he studied how imitation plays a role in social learning.[9] Although he did not state it explicitly, Miller used ordinal position as a factor inasmuch as he pointed out that younger children in the family imitate the older ones. However, in 1937 Murphy, Murphy, and Newcomb in *Experimental Social Psychology*, reviewed about 50 studies on the topic of ordinal position.[10] Their essential conclusion was that the results of these studies on the relationship between birth order and a number of characteristics such as intelligence, school performance, happiness, and emotional stability were inconsistent and contradictory.

Since social psychology has been influenced by the depth psychologies, it is of interest to examine the history of this concept in psychoanalysis. Although the psychoanalysts have never been interested in the relationship of birth order to intelligence, they were once very interested in its relationship to personality. Following Freud's original interest in the influence of childhood factors upon the personality, Alfred Adler contributed many good clinical descriptions of the first, middle, and last born personalities.[11] Both before and after his split with the Freudian school in 1911, he used these descriptions to support his theory of inferiority-superiority. At present, the Adlerians are the only depth psychologists who are interested in birth order. However, probably because of the narrowness of their theory of personality and their alienation from the main rich body of Freudian theory, the Adlerians have contributed no new insights about birth order.

There is no doubt that Adler's leaving the Freudian ranks accounts for most of the formal disinterest by psychoanalysts in the subject of birth order. But the formal neglect does not carry over to the actual work and study of psychoanalysts. In every diagnostic evaluation and in every prolonged treatment, they have an opportunity to witness the effects of birth order. Furthermore, Freud himself never denied its importance. In fact, in his

Introductory Lectures, first written five years after Adler split off, he wrote,

Forced into second place by the birth of another child and for the first time almost entirely parted from the mother, the child finds it very hard to forgive her for this exclusion of him. . . . A child's position in the sequence of brothers and sisters is of very great significance for the course of his later life, a factor to be considered in every biography.[12]

The contrast between the formal and informal attitudes is clearly seen in the writings of Ernest Jones. His adherence to formal theory is illustrated in his book, *Hamlet and Oedipus.*[13] Here he suggests that Hamlet's delay in avenging the murder of his father stems from the same conflict that afflicted Oedipus who unknowingly killed his father and married his mother. He further speculates that Shakespeare wrote Hamlet at this time of his life because Shakespeare's father had recently died. In other words, his father's death reactivated Shakespeare's Oedipus complex.

Jones, in effect, accounted for the *content* of Shakespeare's creativity rather than for the creativity itself. He does not utilize the fact that Shakespeare was his mother's oldest son. However, when Jones wrote his biography of Freud in the 1950's, his informal position on birth order becomes evident when he utilizes Freud's birth order to explain Freud's creativity.

We can gather that [Freud] appears to have been a normal sturdy child and we can note the few features that distinguish his circumstances from those of the average run of children. They are few, but important. He was the eldest child, at least of his mother, and for a time therefore the center of what may be called the inner family. This is in itself a fact of significance, since an eldest child differs, for better or worse, from other children. It may give such a child a special sense of importance and responsibility. . . . He had a veritable passion to understand [his losing his mother to his father and to subsequent siblings]. . . . His intelligence was given a task from which he never flinched until, fifty years later, he found the solution in a fashion that made his name immortal.[14]

We have devoted considerable space to the history of the birth order concept in order to determine whether there are sufficient reasons for the relegation of this factor to the far background. In our opinion there are *not* good reasons. Rather, it appears that birth order, like other scientific ideas, went into comparative oblivion because it could not explain everything or because it was no longer advocated by investigators of authority and repute. The writer cannot speak for the other disciplines, but in regard to psychoanalysis, he wonders if it would not be fruitful to retrieve birth order from the exclusive possession of the Adlerians, examine it systematically, and assign it a proper balanced position in their theory.

In the historical survey we have not dwelt on the actual evidence supporting the birth order hypothesis. This omission we would like to rectify now. At least three rigorous studies suggest a close relationship between birth order and certain aspects of the personality. Their pertinence is more to the characteristics of the ego than to learning per se. But since ego psychology bears on learning, these studies are indirectly pertinent to our major topic.

The first study is by MacArthur, a social anthropologist. The Study of Human Development at Harvard University investigated personality characteristics of first-born and second-born children (families of two children) in two generations—the Harvard graduate and his children. In answering the question of which items "stood up best over two generations," MacArthur states,

For the first children: sensitive, adult oriented, good, conscientious, serious, fearful, and studious are the most reliable in about that order. For the second children, *not studious*, was overwhelmingly common, cheerful and placid stood up pretty well, and there is some tendency to be easy going. All four of these second-child traits reach statistical significance for combined generations. Among the first-child traits, only *serious* and *adult oriented* do so. . . . In most comparisons the first children with siblings turned out to be like the 29 only children in the study.[15]

MacArthur ventures the thought that this latter finding argues against hypothesis that the first-born's personality arises as a reaction to the birth of the sibling rival.

The second study is by Helen Koch who, like MacArthur, investigated families with only two children. She was especially interested in the relationship between the two siblings. She found that second-born children wished their siblings out of the way more frequently than did first born.

Older brothers were more frequently persona non grata. In contrast to the second born, first born who are themselves in the driver's seat, are relatively less disturbed by the interference of these younger sibs and think life can be pleasant with the latter in it. Their affect or hostility is focused more on the parent. Second born and especially boys expressed more frequently than did first born the wish to become the sibling, giving the reason usually that the sib's status, privileges, strength, and knowledge were coveted. . . . We have much evidence that first born, especially boys, were more dependent on the mother, less able to take care of themselves in quarrels with their peers, more competitive, insistent on their rights, and more concerned about their status.

Koch found no marked differences in the intelligence of first- and second-borns though she found the second-born to have a slight advantage.[16, 17]

The third study is the most recent and is reported by Schachter in his *Psychology of Affiliation*. He was investigating in college girls the question of why, in the face of anxiety-producing situations, some girls prefer to be together, whereas others prefer to be alone. More by accident than design, he discovered that under such circumstances, first-born children, more than the later-born, prefer the company of other humans in order to reduce their anxiety. Schachter's surprise at this unexpected relationship is indicative of current expert opinion about ordinal position, and should be quoted.

If at any point the reader has detected a note of astonishment in this recital of the factors of ordinal position, he has been correct, because we have been rather startled by the magnitude and strength of the experimental differences and truly astonished by the apparent generalizibility of these findings of laboratory-experiments conducted on college girls to male alcoholics, World War II veterans in psychotherapy, and jet pilots in the Korean war.[18]

The last bit of evidence comes not from a study but from the pen of a universally acknowledged master psychologist, Dostoevsky. It supports the observations made by others and by the writer. In his *The Brothers Karamazov*, there is an excellent description of older and younger sons. Ivan and Aloysha are the older and younger sons of their father's second marriage. Dimitri, the oldest brother, by a previous marriage, was sent away before their birth. The following description of Ivan is rather typical of many first-born sons of mothers; that of Aloysha, many last-born children.

Dostoevsky writes:

Of the older, Ivan, I will only say that he grew into a somewhat morose and reserved, although far from timid boy. This boy began very early, almost in his infancy . . . to show a brilliant and unusual aptitude for learning. . . . The young man had an unmistakable influence over his father who positively appeared to be ready at times to obey his son.[19]

These characteristics are rather typical of the first-born who, in his serious overmaturity is more leaned upon than leaning.

In contrast is the description of the ingenuous and child-like Aloysha.

Though he lost his mother in his fourth year he remembered her all his life . . . her face, her caresses. [Aloysha] is perhaps the only man in the world you could leave alone without a penny . . . for he would be fed and sheltered at once. . . . It was very characteristic of him, indeed, that he never cared at whose expense he was living. . . . In that respect he was in contrast to his older brother Ivan who maintained himself by his own efforts . . . and [who was] bitterly conscious of living at the expense of his benefactor.[20]

In summary, then, much evidence suggests that birth order does influence the formation of the personality, does in part determine how the ego integrates and handles the inner impulses and the outer environment. It will be recalled that earlier in this chapter we stated that most evidence points to the mother as being highly influential in determining the kind of ego the child develops. Since birth order may reflect different kinds of emotional investment of the mother in her several children, we should not be surprised that it has something to do with individual differences in ego psychology.

The question, of what the direct relationship of birth order to learning and creativity is, remains, however. The only clue supplied by the personality studies was that the first-born children are inclined to be more studious than are the later-born. Though the question must be left unanswered at this time, investigations of atypical samples by the author suggest that birth order is related to the *quality* of creativity rather than to its *quantity*. Report of these investigations will be made at some future time.

C

NOTE: All figures shown in the following tables are significant to the 0.5 level of significance unless they are noted as *subsignificant* (in the direction of the hypothesis, but not significant to the 0.5 level) or *non-significant* (showing no significant difference and not tending in the direction of the hypothesis). (See Appendix A, p. 174.)

Table I—Relation of Father's Occupation and Education to Son's Learning

Group	Father Professional or College Educated	Father Skilled or High School Graduate	Father Semiskilled or Not High School Graduate	Father Insufficient Data	Number
			(per cent)		
Learners	48	31	15	6	100
Non-learners	17	33	42	8	100

* The percentage differences for "father skilled or high school graduate" are *subsignificant*.

Table II—Relation of Father's Occupation and Education to Particular Learning Difficulties in the Son

Groups	Father's Occupation and Education	I.Q. Below 106	I.Q. Above 105	Working to Capacity	Repeated at least One Grade	Number
				(per cent)		
Learners	Professional or college ed.	21	79	84	0	48
	Skilled or high school grad.	29	71	74	0	31
	Semiskiled or Semiskilled or not high school grad.	60	40	87	0	15
Non-Learners	Professional or college ed.	35	65	12	18	17
	Skilled or high school grad.	45	55	30	30	33
	Semiskilled or not high school grad.	69	31	59	67	42

* The percentage differences for learners under "working to capacity" are *non-significant*.

[186]

Table III—Relation of Family Size to Intelligence Scores

Group	Family Size	I.Q. below 106	I.Q. above 105	Number
		(per cent)		
Learners	No more than 3 children	23	77	64
	More than 3 children	56	44	36
Non-Learners	No more than 3 children	27	73	62
	More than 3 children	71	29	38

Table IV—Relation of Family Size to Intelligence Scores in Clinic Boys and Girls

Sex	Family Size	INTELLIGENCE LEVEL Dull or Below	Average	High Average or Above	Number
		(per cent)			
Boys	No more than 3 children	29	37	34	1544
	More than 3 children	43	41	16	540
Girls	No more than 3 children	31	37	32	502
	More than 3 children	51	40	9	171

* The percentage differences under "average" intelligence level are *non-significant*.

Table V—Relation of Family Size to School-Leaving in Military Psychiatric Patients

Family Size	Not Finishing High School	Finishing High School Only	Entering College	Number
		(per cent)		
No more than 3 children	54	24	22	179
4 to 5 children	67	18	15	120
More than 5 children	80	16	4	225

Table VI—Relation of Ethnic Group to Learning

Ethnic Group	Learners	Non-learners	Number
	(per cent)		
Jewish	70	30	46
Non-Jewish	44	56	154

Table VII—Relation of Ethnic Group to Learning Manifestations

Group	Ethnic Group	I.Q. below 106	I.Q. above 105	Repeated at least One Grade	Number
			(per cent)		
Learners	Jewish	25	75	0	32
	Non-Jewish	38	62	0	68
Non-	Jewish	36	64	21	14
Learners	Non-Jewish	49	51	56	86

* The percentage differences under "I.Q." headings are *subsignificant*.

Table VIII—Relation of Learning Problems in Younger and Older Boys to Double Family Disorganization (Marital Discord and Mother Working)

Age	Group	Have Double Family Disorganization	Number
		(per cent)	
Below ten	Learners	12	51
	Non-learners	29	52
Ten and above	Learners	6	49
	Non-learners	10	48
All	Learners	9	100
	Non-learners	20	100

* All percentages shown are *subsignificant* except those for "all" learners and "all" non-learners, which are significant.

Table IX—Relation of Family Disorganization to Learning Difficulties in Boys Below Ten

Group	Family Disor-ganization	Not Work-ing to Capacity	LEARNING DIFFICULTIES Difficulty in Concen-trating	Repeated Grade	Reading Difficulty	Num-ber
			(per cent)			
Learners	None	25	10	0	0	20
	Single	32	16	0	0	25
	Double	50	50	0	0	6
Non-Learners	None	80	60	40	44	25
	Single	92	67	58	58	12
	Double	80	93	67	67	15

NOTE: Single disorganization means that there is *either* the mother working or marital discord in the home. Double disorganization means that there is *both* the mother working and marital discord in the home.

* Percentage differences for non-learners under "not working to capacity" are *non-significant*.

Table X—Relation of Maternal Ambition to Intelligence Test Scores

Mother Ambi-tious	Group	I.Q. below 110	I.Q. 110-119	I.Q. 120 and above	Num-ber
			(per cent)		
No	Learners	33	36	31	76
	Non-learners	66	11	23	65
Yes	Learners	21	37	42	24
	Non-learners	60	29	11	35

* The percentage difference between learners and non-learners with I.Q.'s of 110-119 who have ambitious mothers is *non-significant*. The percentage difference between learners and non-learners with I.Q.'s of 120 and above who do not have ambitious mothers is also *non-significant*.

Table XI—Relation of Maternal Ambition to Other Learning Symptoms

Group	Mother Ambitious	Not Working to Capacity	Repeated Grade	Number
		(per cent)		
Learners	No	28	0	76
	Yes	54	0	24
Non-Learners	No	88	55	65
	Yes	80	37	35

* All percentages are *significant* except for those under both "not working to capacity" for non-learners and "repeated grade" for learners—which are *non-significant*.

Table XII—Relation of Maternal Pressure to Son's "Slowness" in Non-learners

Maternal Pressure	"Son Is Slow" (per cent)	Number
None	17	29
Some	24	58
Much	61	13

Table XIII—Relation of Birth Order to Learning Problems

Group	Only Child	First Born	Middle Born	Last Born	Number
			(per cent)		
Learners	13	57	14	16	100
Non-learners	18	33	21	28	100

* The percentage differences under "only child" and "middle born" are *non-significant*.

Table XIV—Relation of Birth Order to Learning and Personality Characteristics in Clinic Children from Families of Two or Three Children

Sex	Birth Order	Immature	Slow	Bright (per cent)	I.Q. below 90	I.Q. above 109	Number
Male	First born	21	12	70	27	34	868
	Last born	31	13	35	27	32	451
Female	First born	22	11	7	27	37	309
	Last born	28	20	6	40	21	181

* The following figures are *subsignificant:* (1) those under "immature" for females; (2) those under "bright" for males. The following figures are *non-significant* (1) those under "I.Q. below 90" for males; (2) those under "I.Q. above 109" for males; (3) those under "bright" for females.

Table XV—Relation of Mother's Working to Serious Outlook of First and Last Born Sons

Group	Mother Works	Birth Order	School Says Boy Is "Serious" (per cent)	Number
Learners	No	First born	13	39
		Last born	18	11
	Yes	First born	27	18
		Last born	0	5
Non-learners	No	First born	13	17
		Last born	8	12
	Yes	First born	50	16
		Last born	6	16
Both	No	First born	13	56
		Last born	13	23
	Yes	First born	38	34
		Last born	5	21

* The percentage difference for first and last born learners whose mothers do not work is *non-significant*, and that for first and last born non-learners whose mothers do not work is *subsignificant*.

Table XVI—Relation of Birth Order and Marital Discord to Development Problems

Birth Order	Group	Marital Discord	Feeding Problems	Enuresis	Number
			(per cent)		
First born	Learners	No	13	26	34
		Yes	29	29	23
	Non-learners	No	25	20	20
		Yes	54	23	13
Last born	Learners	No	10	10	10
		Yes	33	67	6
	Non-learners	No	7	13	15
		Yes	8	60	13
First born	Learners	All	19	26	57
Last born	Learners	All	13	25	16
First born	Non-learners	All	36	21	33
Last born	Non-learners	All	11	39	28

* The following percentage differences are *subsignificant*: (1) those for first born and last born learners under "feeding problems"; (2) those for learners and non-learners when marital discord is not considered ("all") under "enuresis."
The following percentage differences are *non-significant*: (1) those for last born non-learners under "feeding problems"; (2) those for first born and last born learners when marital discord is not considered ("all") under "feeding problems"; (3) those for first born learners and non-learners when marital discord is considered under "enuresis."

Table XVII—*Relation of Mother's Projection of Blame and Marital Compatibility to Son's Behavior in School*

Group	Marital Compatibility	Mother Blames Others for Boy's Problems	Clearly Submissive	Clearly Aggressive	Number
			BOY'S CLASSROOM BEHAVIOR		
			(per cent)		
Learners	Compatible	No	28	18	39
		Yes	18	62	18
	Incompatible	No	35	30	20
		Yes	9	43	23
Non-Learners	Compatible	No	11	26	34
		Yes	39	35	23
	Incompatible	No	69	31	13
		Yes	27	50	30
	Compatible	No	34	22	73
		Yes	29	44	41
	Incompatible	No	48	30	33
		Yes	19	49	53

Table XVIII—*Relation of Aggressive and Non-Aggressive Behavior to Learning Problems*

Group	Submissive	Co-operative	Sometimes Openly Aggressive	Number
		CLASSROOM BEHAVIOR		
		(per cent)		
Learners	23	32	45	100
Non-learners	40	3	57	100

Table XIX—*Relation of Aggression to Intelligence in Non-Learners*

Classroom Behavior	I.Q. 110 and above (per cent)	Number
Clearly submissive	15	40
Clearly aggressive	43	37

Table XX—Relation of Aggressive Behavior to Ability to Work to Capacity

Group	Classroom Behavior	Not Working to Capacity (per cent)	Number
Learners	Not clearly aggressive	7	67
	Clearly aggressive	45	33
Non-learners	Not clearly aggressive	54	63
	Clearly aggressive	81	37

Table XXI—Relation of Aggression to Intelligence in Learners

Classroom Behavior	I.Q. below 110	I.Q. 110-119 (per cent)	I.Q. 120 and above	Number
Co-operative	27	33	40	30
Clearly aggressive	39	28	33	33

* All percentage differences shown are non-significant.

Table XXII—Relation of Aggression to Reading Difficulties in Non-Learners

Classroom Behavior	Reading Difficulties (per cent)	Number
Clearly submissive	75	40
Mixed	26	23
Clearly aggressive	57	37

Table XXIII—Relation of Reading Problems to Aggression and Constipation in Non-Learners

Reading Problems	Classroom Behavior	History of Constipation (per cent)	Number
Present	Clearly submissive	47	30
Present	Clearly aggressive	18	11

NOTE: *Complete references to all articles and books noted below will be found in the Bibliography, pp. 203-206.*

Chapter I

1. Beveridge, W. I. B., *The Art of Scientific Investigation,* pp. 33-35.
2. Plato, *Republic,* Book VII.

Chapter II

3. Davis, Alison and Havighurst, Robert, "Social Class and Color Difference in Child Rearing." Bossard, James, *The Sociology of Child Development.*
4. Brossard, *op. cit.,* p. 184.
5. Davis and Havighurst, *op. cit.*
6. Hollingshead, A. B., *Elmstown's Youth,* p. 331.
7. Heintz, Emil, "Adjustment Problems of Class Status."

Chapter III

8. Harris, Irving, *Normal Children and Mothers,* pp. 101-10.
9. Freud, Anna and Burlingham, Dorothy, *Infants without Families.*
10. Robinson, Helen, *Why Pupils Fail in Reading.*

Chapter IV

11. Toynbee, Arnold, *Study of History,* p. 140.

Chapter V

12. Harris, Irving, *op. cit.,* pp. 137-47.

Chapter X

13. Hilgard, Ernest, *Theories of Learning,* p. 486.
14. Freud, Sigmund, *The Problem of Anxiety,* pp. 11-16.
15. Pearson, G. H. J., *Psychoanalysis and the Education of the Child.*

16. Abraham, Karl, *Selected Papers on Psychoanalysis*, pp. 169-234.

17. Strachey, J., "Some Unconscious Factors in Reading."

18. Jarvis, J., "Clinical Observations on Visual Problems in Reading Disability," and Rosen, J., "Strephosymbolia."

19. Hilgard, *loc. cit.*

20. Spitz, R., "Anxiety in Infancy."

21. Rank, Beata, "Aggression," in Ruth S. Eissler, *et al.*, III/IV, 43.

22. Freud, Anna, "Aggression in Relation to Emotional Development," in Ruth E. Eissler, *et al.*, III/IV, p. 41.

23. Kris, Ernst, "Neutralization and Sublimation," in Ruth S. Eissler, *et al.*, X, 45.

24. Robinson, Helen, *op. cit.*

25. Fabian, A., "Reading Disability: An Index of Pathology," p. 326.

26. Mowrer, O. H., *Learning Theory and Personality Dynamics*, p. 700.

27. Harlow, H., "A Theory of the Development of Affection in Primates."

28. Harris, Irving D., *op. cit.*, p. 15.

29. Hilgard, *op. cit.*, p. 457.

Chapter XI

30. Freud, Anna, *Introduction to Psychoanalysis for Teachers*, pp. 10-11.

31. Rivlin, H., "Round Table: Contemporary Concepts of Learning," pp. 776, 781.

32. Highet, Gilbert, *The Art of Teaching*, p. 18.

33. *Ibid.*, p. 25.

34. *Ibid.*, p. 36.

35. *Ibid.*, p. 41.

36. *Ibid.*, p. 48.

37. *Ibid.*, p. 57.

38. Harris, Irving, *op. cit.*, p. 169

39. Engler, D., *How To Raise Your Child's I.Q.* See the dust jacket.

40. Pearson, G. H. J., *op. cit.*, p. 215.
p. 215.

41. Anderson, H. H. (ed.), *Creativity and Its Cultivation*.

42. Stoddard, G., "Creativity in Education," in *ibid.*, p. 187.

43. Mead, Margaret, "Creativity in Cross-Cultural Perspective," in *ibid.*,

44. *Ibid.*

45. Fromm, Erich, "The Creative Attitude," in *ibid.*, p. 52.

46. Eyring, H., "Scientific Creativity," in *ibid.*, p. 4.

47. Hilgard, Ernest, "Creativity and Problem Solving," in *ibid.*, pp. 170-71.

48. *Ibid.*, p. 177.

Appendix

1. Cronbach, Lee J., *Educational Psychology*.

2. Lindgren, Henry C., *Mental Health in Education*.

3. Redl, Fritz and Wattenberg, William, *Mental Hygiene in Learning*.

Notes   [199]

4. Galton, F., *English Men of Science, Their Nature and Nurture.*
5. Ellis, H., *A Study of British Genius.*
6. Cattell J. McK., "Families of American Men of Science."
7. Terman, Lewis M., *Mental and Physical Traits of a Thousand Gifted Children.*
8. Jones, H., "The Environment and Mental Development," in L. Carmichael (ed.) *Manual of Child Psychology,* p. 668.
9. Miller, Neal and Dollard, John, *Social Learning and Imitation.*
10. Murphy, G., Murphy, L., and Newcomb, T., *Experimental Social Psychology.*
11. Adler, Alfred, *The Education of Children.*
12. Freud, Sigmund, *A General Introduction to Psychoanalysis,* p. 293.
13. Jones, Ernest, *Hamlet and Oedipus.*
14. Jones, Ernest, *The Life and Work of Sigmund Freud,* pp. 13-14.
15. MacArthur, C., "Personalities of First and Second Children," p. 49.
16. Koch, Helen, *Human Development Bulletin, Fifth Annual Symposium,* pp. 1-3.
17. Koch, Helen, "Some Personality Correlates of Sex, Sibling Position, and Sex of Sibling Among Five- and Six-Year-Old Children," in *ibid.*
18. Schacter, Stanley, *The Psychology of Affiliation,* p. 78.
19. Dostoevsky, Fyodor, *The Brothers Karamazov,* p. 13.
20. *Ibid.,* pp. 16, 19-20.

BIBLIOGRAPHY

Abraham, Karl. *Selected Papers on Psychoanalysis*. London: Hogarth Press, 1949.

Adler, Alfred. *The Education of Children*. New York: Greenberg, 1930.

Anderson, H. H. *Creativity and Its Cultivation*. New York: Harper & Bros., 1957.

Beveridge, W. I. B. *The Art of Scientific Investigation*. New York: Random House, 1950.

Bossard, James. *The Sociology of Child Development*. New York: Harper & Bros., 1948.

Cattell, J. McK. "Families of American Men of Science, III: Vital Statistics and Composition of the Families," *Scientific Monthly*, V (1917), 368-77.

Cronbach, Lee J. *Educational Psychology*. New York: Harcourt Brace, 1954.

Davis, Alison and Havighurst, Robert. "Social Class and Color Differences in Child Rearing," *American Sociological Review*, XII (1946), 698-710.

Dostoevsky, Fyodor. *The Brothers Karamazov*. New York: Modern Library, 1950.

Ellis, H. *A Study of British Genius*. London: Hurst & Blackett, 1904.

Engler, David. *How to Raise Your Child's IQ*. New York: Criterion, 1958.

Eyring, H. "Scientific Creativity" in H. H. Anderson (ed.). *Creativity and Its Cultivation*. New York: Harper & Bros., 1957.

Fabian, A. "Reading Disability: An Index of Pathology," *American Journal of Orthopsychiatry*, XXV (1955), 326.

Freud, Anna. "Aggression in Relation to Emotional Development: Normal and Pathological," in Ruth S. Eissler, *et al.* (eds.). *Psychoanalytic Study of the Child*. New York: International Universities Press, 1949. III/IV, 37-42.

———. *Introduction to Psychoanalysis for Teachers*. London: Allen & Unwin, 1931.

——— and Burlingham, Dorothy. *Infants without Families*. New York: International Universities Press, 1944.

Freud, Sigmund. *A General Introduction to Psychoanalysis*. New
        York: Liveright, 1933.
————. *The Problem of Anxiety*. New York: W. W. Norton, 1936.
Fromm, Erich. "The Creative Attitude," in H. H. Anderson (ed.).
        Creativity and Its Cultivation. New York: Harper & Bros.
Galton, F. *English Men of Science, Their Nature and Nurture*.
        London: Macmillan, 1874.
Harlow, H. "A Theory of the Development of Affection in Pri-
        mates." Unpublished manuscript.
Harris, Irving. *Normal Children and Mothers*. Glencoe, Ill.: The
        Free Press, 1959.
Heintz, Emil. "Adjustment Problems of Class Status," *Phi Delta
        Kappan*, XXX (1949), 290-93.
Highet, Gilbert. *The Art of Teaching*. New York: Vintage Books,
        1958.
Hilgard, Ernest R. "Creativity and Problem Solving," in H. H.
        Anderson (ed.). *Creativity and Its Cultivation*. New York:
        Harper & Bros., 1957.
————. *Theories of Learning*. New York: Appleton-Century-Crofts,
        1956.
Hollingshead, A. B. *Elmstown's Youth*. New York: J. Wiley & Sons,
        1949.
Jarvis, J. "Clinical Observations on the Visual Problem in Reading
        Disability," in Ruth S. Eissler, *et al.* (eds.). *Psychoanalytic
        Study of the Child*. New York: International Universities
        Press, 1958. XIII, 451-70.
Jones, Ernest. *Hamlet and Oedipus*. Garden City, N. Y.: Double-
        day, 1954.
————. *The Life and Work of Sigmund Freud*, Vol. I. New York:
        Basic Books, 1953.
Jones, H. "The Environment and Mental Development," in L. Car-
        michael (ed.). *Manual of Child Psychology*. New York: J.
        Wiley & Sons, 1946.
Koch, H. *Human Development Bulletin, Fifth Annual Symposium*.
        Chicago: University of Chicago Press.
————. "Some Personality Correlates of Sex, Sibling Position, and
        Sex of Sibling among Five- and Six-Year-Old Children,"
        Genetic Psychology Monographs, LII (1955), 3-50.
Kris, Ernst. "Neutralization and Sublimation," in Ruth S. Eissler,
        et al. (eds.). *Psychoanalytic Study of the Child*. New York:
        International Universities Press, 1953. X, 30-46.

Lindgren, Henry C. *Mental Health in Education*. New York: Henry Holt, 1954.

MacArthur, C. "Personalities of First and Second Children," *Psychiatry*, Vol. XIX (1956).

Mead, Margaret. "Creativity in Cross-Cultural Perspective," in H. H. Anderson (ed.). *Creativity and Its Cultivation*. New York: Harper & Bros., 1957.

Miller, Neal and Dollard, John. *Social Learning and Imitation*. New Haven: Yale University Press, 1941.

Mowrer, O. H. *Learning Theory and Personality Dynamics*. New York: Ronald Press, 1950.

Murphy, G., Murphy, L., and Newcomb, T. *Experimental Social Psychology*. New York: Harper & Bros., 1937.

Pearson, G. H. J. *Psychoanalysis and the Education of the Child*. New York: W. W. Norton, 1954.

Rank, Beata. "Aggression," in Ruth S. Eissler, et al. (eds.). *The Psychoanalytic Study of the Child*. New York: International Universities Press, 1949. III/IV, 43.

Redl, Fritz and Wattenberg, William. *Mental Hygiene in Teaching*. New York: Harcourt, Brace, 1951.

Redlich, Frederick C. and Hollingshead, August B. *Social Classes and Mental Illness*. New York: J. Wiley & Sons, 1958.

Rivlin, Harry N. "Round Table: Contemporary Concepts of Learning," *American Journal of Orthopsychiatry*, XXIV (1954), 767-88.

Robinson, Helen. *Why Pupils Fail in Reading*. Chicago: University of Chicago Press, 1954.

Rosen, V. "Strephosymbolia: An Intrasystemic Disturbance of the Synthetic Function of the Ego," in Ruth S. Eissler, et al. (eds.). *Psychoanalytic Study of the Child*. New York: International Universities Press, 1955. X, 83-99.

Schacter, Stanley. *The Psychology of Affiliation*. Stanford, Calif.: Stanford University Press, 1959.

Spitz, René. "Anxiety in Infancy," *International Journal of Psychoanalysis*, XXXI (1950), 138-47.

Stoddard, G. "Creativity in Education," in H. H. Anderson (ed.). *Creativity and Its Cultivation*. New York: Harper & Bros., 1957.

Strachey, J. "Some Unconscious Factors in Reading," *International Journal of Psychoanalysis*, XI (1930), 322-31.

Terman, Lewis M. *Mental and Physical Traits of a Thousand*

Bibliography

Gifted Children (*Genetic Studies of Genius*, L. Terman (ed.) Vol. I). Stanford, Calif.: Stanford University Press, 1925.

Toynbee, Arnold. *A Study of History*. Abridgement of Vols. I-XI, D. C. Somervell (ed.). New York and London: Oxford University Press, 1947, 1957.